The Happy Teacher Habits

Also by Michael Linsin:

Classroom Management for Art, Music, and PE Teachers

The Classroom Management Secret

Dream Class

The Happy Teacher Habits

11 Habits of the Happiest, Most Effective Teachers on Earth

Michael Linsin

Printed in the USA

JME Publishing
San Diego, California
smartclassroommanagement.com

Copy Editor
Laura Decorte

Proofreaders
Christine Haack
Scott Herring
Mike Mckown

Note: In a small number of cases, names have been changed and situations altered to protect the identity of those known to the author.

ISBN: 0692659242
ISBN: 9780692659243

Table of Contents

Flow: A highly pleasurable mental state in which you're fully immersed in a feeling of energized focus, full involvement, and enjoyment in an activity. You lose yourself in the moment, concerns and worries of the past and future fade away, and your performance soars.

Narrow

I n 2008, Jess Lee was a 26-year-old product manager at Google who in her free time liked to peruse a fashion website called Polyvore. Lee had grown up in Hong Kong and dreamed of being a comic book writer and artist. She loved the creative aspects of Polyvore and how it allowed users to mix and match outfits right on the site, like a high-tech version of paper dolls. She also enjoyed following other users whose style profiles she admired.

One day on a whim she sent a long and detailed email to Pasha Sadri, one of the founders of Polyvore, to suggest ways he might improve the site. Intrigued, Sadri wrote back and asked her to meet him for coffee. By the end of the meeting, Sadri had offered Lee a job. By 2012, Lee was CEO of the company. In just a few short years, she had taken Polyvore, as well as Silicon Valley, by storm by applying her version of what is known as the 80/20 rule.

The 80/20 rule was the brainchild of economist and mathematician Vilfredo Pareto, who in 1906 observed that 80 percent of the land wealth in Italy was owned by just 20 percent of the population. This distribution has often been described as a universal law that is as predictable and provable as the law of gravity. The rule states that 20 percent of inputs tend to produce 80 percent of the outputs.

It's important to point out that the percentages are rough estimates only and don't always add up to 100 percent. For example, 5 percent of your students may account for 99 percent of the misbehavior in your class. 27 percent of real estate agents in your area may be responsible for selling 84 percent of the properties. 19 percent of the clothing in your wardrobe may be worn 68 percent of the time.

The point of the 80/20 rule is that in virtually every industry or endeavor, just a few things make the greatest difference. The rule has also been called "the vital few and the trivial many" and "Pareto's Principle." It can be a powerful way to improve performance in everything from sports to business to education. In the 1950s, a management consultant named Joseph Juran famously used the rule to help improve Japan's manufacturing industries, which by the 1980s became a leader in producing high quality products like automobiles and televisions.

When Jess Lee began working at Polyvore, she identified those few areas that had the most impact on moving the business forward, and resolved to do them exceedingly well. She cut popular features and eliminated distractions in order to double down on the vital few efforts that resulted in the greatest growth. She simplified, streamlined, and narrowed in on the 20 percent (or so) that mattered most to Polyvore's success.

The website grew. It now has over 20 million unique visitors per month and has been profitable since 2012. If you go to Polyvore.com and navigate to the Team page, you'll discover that "do a few things well" is one of the core values at Polyvore. It's also the secret behind some of the most successful companies in the world, including Apple, Google, Twitter, Starbucks, and Berkshire-Hathaway, who all focus on doing just a few things well.

But the application of the 80/20 rule extends far beyond businesses and organizations. Individuals like artists, writers, lawyers, and athletes have long used the 80/20 rule to improve their efficiency, productivity, and performance. By identifying the 20 percent of efforts that matter most and produce the greatest results, anyone can save time, improve performance, and simplify their life. Anyone can de-emphasize the non-essentials, or cut them out altogether, and limit their tasks to what is most important to their success and fulfillment. Teachers, too, can use the 80/20 rule to lower their stress and improve their job satisfaction, as well as the results they're getting in the classroom.

Discovering the 20 percent can be life-changing. The problem with applying the rule to teaching, however, is that education is a sea of confusing and conflicting philosophies, strategies, and methods. It's rife with change and complexity and an overwhelming amount of information. Therefore, it can be difficult to identify what is most vital to your success. It can also be a challenge to apply the 80/20 rule when you're expressly told by your administrator, and through your curriculum, what to teach and when to teach it.

When I was a young teacher in the early 1990s, I can remember being unhappy with the district-adopted reading program that emphasized an approach called "whole language." So I knocked on the principal's door and asked if I could have the funds to purchase my own materials. She was happy to oblige. So while many of my colleagues were teaching reading through sight words, I was teaching something entirely different. And this was acceptable, even applauded.

I was also given free rein to decide what units I would teach each month and the pace I would follow. Although I was guided by a curriculum, I decided how and when it would be fulfilled, along with what materials I thought were best suited to my students. It felt very much like being my own boss. I could indulge my creative instincts. I could choose to give my students a break when they needed it. I could teach an art lesson first thing in the morning or head outside for some exercise after lunch. I was a trusted professional who knew what was best for my students.

Nowadays, such freedom is long gone and will likely never return. We are now informed exactly what content must be taught and when. We're given precise timelines and schedules and even instructed on what we should have displayed on our classroom walls. Month after month, we attend inservice trainings and meetings where we're presented with more and more new strategies, methods, and approaches in a way that suggests that all of it is equally important. Well, as we know from the 80/20 rule, it's not. Not even close. The truth is most of it is unimportant, if not irrelevant.

Yet, we feel pressured to do it all. We feel pressured to squeeze it all in. We keep adding and adding as the stress level goes up and up. The job gets bigger and more complicated and confusing every year, with no end in sight. Every staff meeting fills us with anxiety over what new procedure or program must now be added to the list. The constant change leads to feelings of unpreparedness, inadequacy, and low confidence, which, particularly at lower performing schools, can be especially draining.

This combination of having less freedom and less say about how we do our job, along with the endless flow of information and responsibilities heaped onto our teaching plate, causes more and more teachers to burn out. It causes more and more teachers to resent their job and the toll it takes on their family and personal life. Stress and low morale are rampant in the profession. Between 40 and 50 percent of teachers leave the classroom within five years, with nine and a half percent leaving before their first year is even finished.

Never in 25 years of teaching have I witnessed so many unhappy teachers. Never have I witnessed so many overworked, stressed-out, and exhausted teachers. With so much to do, and with misbehavior and disrespect seemingly on the rise, teachers are feeling trapped. They're feeling resigned to a job that once held such promise, but is now an albatross around their neck. The dream of inspiring a room full of eager students who listen, behave, and *want* to learn is a distant memory, chalked up to silly innocence and naïveté.

In response, caring teachers do the only thing they can think of to do: They work harder. They get up earlier. They stay later. They toss and turn in bed at night, mulling over how they're going to tackle another monumental list of problems and challenges awaiting them in the morning. They prepare and grade papers in the evenings and on the weekends. They fight the good fight and endure the emotional wear and tear it takes on them and their loved ones. They give and give and give some more.

While it's true that hard work is a critical ingredient to success, there is a point of diminishing returns—in every profession. There is a point where you're actually worse off by working harder.

Long distance runners know that if they cross this threshold, their performance will suffer dramatically. Their chances of injury and sickness will rise. They'll experience depression, lack of appetite, and sleep disturbances. They'll grow anxious and irritable. And that's just from overdoing it physically. Emotional strain can be even more debilitating, to the degree of not wanting to get out of bed in the morning.

In teaching, the point where working harder becomes a detriment comes quickly. It comes fast and furious because, perhaps more than any other profession, teaching requires you to be at your best. It requires you to be fresh and rested. It requires you to be mentally sharp and patient and *passionate* about your work. It requires you to be relaxed, calm, and acutely aware of your surroundings.

Like runners who overtrain, teachers who are spread too thin suffer dramatic decreases in performance. They become stressed and impatient. They bring tension into their classroom and cause more misbehavior than any ten students combined. They snap at unruly students and grow increasingly more unlikable. There is also the issue of the 80/20 rule. If you're unsure what 20 percent actually matters to your success, then most of that extra work is in vain. It's like paddling a canoe furiously against a current and getting nowhere.

When I was in middle school, my sister and I were on a swim team. Three nights a week my parents would drop us off at the local pool where we would swim lap after lap. Our coach instructed us to kick and pull through the water as hard as we could. The emphasis was on building strength and endurance by increasing our number of laps or by trying to spin our arms quicker through the water. We also used kickboards to train our legs to flutter harder and faster. There was even a machine alongside the pool that used progressive resistance to build our swimming muscles. By the end of every practice, we were exhausted.

At the time, this was typical of swimming instruction. After receiving initial guidance on how to perform a given stroke, the focus would shift to improving power and fitness through repetitive practice. The idea was that the more you swam, the stronger you got and the smoother and more efficient your form would become.

Then a young swimming coach from New York named Terry Laughlin noticed that a small minority of swimmers were able to swim remarkably fast, but without trying hard. They glided over the water effortlessly and with very little churn in their wake. He wondered if he could somehow teach his students to do the same. So instead of pushing them to do more and more laps, he began teaching them how to swim like "natural swimmers." He focused on perfecting their technique and showing them how to move their torso efficiently. He taught them to be fishlike in their movements and slip through the water rather than muscling through it. The results were stunning.

With far less time in the pool, his students were swimming faster and with less effort than ever before. He discovered that the fastest swimmers actually take fewer strokes than everyone else. He discovered through the work of some of the world's top researchers that only 30 percent of elite-level swimming performance was owed to fitness. For amateur swimmers, the percentage was even less and closer to 10 percent.

It turns out that all that time and hard work devoted to swimming lap after lap is a terribly inefficient way to learn how to swim. It also causes injury, burnout, and scores of people to give up the sport altogether. Laughlin used the 80/20 rule to focus on the vital few details that mattered most in getting from one side of the pool to the other, and in so doing revolutionized swimming instruction. He transformed lap swimming from a grueling exercise to an enjoyable, even meditative, experience. He taught swimmers of all ages how to do less, but get better results.

For many, being a teacher feels like being under the thumb of an old-school swimming instructor. You're told to push harder and faster—perhaps not in so many words, but the message is clear: You need to do more in order to get better results. But it's a lie. Doing more isn't the answer. The answer is doing less. The answer is to focus on the vital 20 percent that has the greatest impact on your effectiveness and personal fulfillment. They are, after all, intertwined. When you love your work, you're naturally going to be more effective. Your students are going to like you a lot more. Your lessons will be more dynamic and you'll have more energy. It becomes a virtuous cycle.

In this book, I'm going to show you how to recapture why you wanted to become a teacher in the first place. I'm going to show you the 20 percent that really matters to your happiness and success and how to double down on it—while de-emphasizing the 80 percent that is stressful and has little value.

I'm going to help you simplify your teaching life down to its essential core and narrow in on the habits employed by the happiest teachers, who remain both highly effective and in love with teaching despite the pressure to do more and work harder. I'm going to show you how to work smarter and more efficiently, so you can leave school at school and spend more time with your family, friends, and the hobbies you enjoy.

I'm also going to teach you the secrets to motivating students and inspiring in them a love of learning. I'm going to give you the keys to planning in half the time and teaching lessons that will cause your students to hang on to your every word. I'm going to take you through each and every strategy in easy-to-understand detail, much the way Terry Laughlin broke down the swimming stroke.

The book is based on my own practice as well as those of the most effective teachers I've known throughout my career. I also leaned on the knowledge I've gained from the thousands of emails I've received from overworked and unhappy teachers. I've condensed everything I know about creating a career you can be proud of into simple, doable strategies that anyone in any teaching situation or grade level can apply.

One important criterion I followed was that each of the strategies had to be timeless. They had to endure through any and every change to education, technology, teaching approach, and the like. They had to be effective yesterday, today, and into the future. They also had to be proven—and not just by me and the many teachers I've coached and mentored, but through research you've likely never heard of before.

I drew on experts from the world of business, marketing, sports, entertainment, music, and medicine. You're going to hear dozens of stories and examples of people applying these strategies and experiencing remarkable success.

Much of what you will learn is likely to be new to you, but don't let that throw you off. They are the most powerful and transformational strategies in teaching, as well as in many careers and activities outside of education. They are what I've relied on for the past 25 years to not only teach effectively, but to love (almost) every minute of it. More importantly, they allow you to have a life outside of school.

When Karina Canellakis performs with a symphony, whether in Dallas where she is an assistant conductor, or in one of the many cities she travels to as a guest, newspaper reviewers often comment that she appears to be having fun on stage. Although she isn't aware of it, she's been told that she even smiles while performing. In an article in *The San Diego Union Tribune*, she said, "It's important to be really in love with what you're performing in order to translate it to the audience in a powerful way." The idea that, among all professions, teachers in particular must be martyrs who tragically throw themselves on the altar of education is not only absurd, but damaging to our students.

It's okay to love your job. It's okay to get your work done and go home to your family. It's okay to like having your summers off. It's okay to care about your students, but not take their issues home with you. I'm sorry if that sounds harsh or selfish, but here's the thing: Although by nature teachers are caring and nurturing souls, those who can put the concerns of the day behind them and recharge their batteries are happier and far more effective than those who take their work home with them and bleed for the job.

Teaching is *supposed* to be rewarding. It's supposed to be fun. It's supposed to be the career you first imagined when you decided to become a teacher. Instead of trying to convince yourself that you like your job, or that you're doing it all for your students, this book will show you how to truly enjoy it. It will show you how to hone in on what really matters and how to do it exceptionally well.

Successful teaching isn't big, complex, and time-consuming. It's small, simple, and efficient. Jess Lee, Joseph Juran, and Terry Laughlin took what was difficult and transformed it into something remarkable by applying the 80/20 rule. It's my sincerest belief and deepest confidence that this book will do the same for you. I invite you to turn the page, open your mind, and change your teaching life forever.

I don't know where I am but I know I don't like it

-General Public, "Tenderness"

"It's only by saying no that you can concentrate
on the things that are really important."

-Steve Jobs

Decline

During my third year of teaching I was asked if I'd like to become an outdoor education trainer for my school district. It was a cool position because my main responsibility was taking teachers into the San Gabriel Mountains near Los Angeles to teach them how to conduct experiments in the field. We'd take temperature and barometer readings. We'd measure the water speed of creeks and waterfalls overflowing with snowmelt. We'd hike for miles while I'd point out rock formations, indigenous plants and trees, and evidence of animal activity. We waded through streams, ate blackberries off the branch, and laid in the grass to listen to the natural world around us.

I would try to capture for them the same glorious experience I wanted them to pass along to their students, who they would then take on the same trip later in the year. I wanted to put them in their students' shoes so that they could *feel* the thrill and enjoyment of being in the wild and away from modernity. My goal was no less than they would have the time of their lives.

I knew that their enthusiasm for the adventure was key to their students having the same memorable experience. I hoped that maybe, just maybe, in one fell swoop it would help change their perspective on the world. By the end of the four-hour hike, they were exhausted, to be sure, but couldn't wipe the smiles off their faces.

I loved being an outdoor education trainer. I made some really good friends and learned a lot about teaching and the importance of immersing students in their learning. It also afforded me other opportunities. Before long, I was traveling from school to school with a portable planetarium. I'd tell mythological stories while pointing out the constellations of Argo Navis and Corona Borealis, Cygnus and Draco, and many others. I told tales of the Southern Cross and the Northern Lights. The subject was so captivating that despite being in a near pitch-black dome, I never once had to warn a student about their behavior.

I also taught classes on composting, airplane flight, and anything else they asked me to do. I said yes to astronomy night, Earth Day, and field trips to the local water plant. I can remember meeting students at four o'clock in the morning to track the space shuttle Endeavor across the night sky. Before I knew it I was saying yes to a parade of teachers stomping through my classroom to watch me teach. I became the GATE (Gifted and Talented Education) coordinator at my school and a new-teacher mentor. I was an advisor for student government. I traveled to additional trainings and seminars. I collaborated, deliberated, discussed, and strategized.

And I was miserable. It was too much. Even the trips to the mountains became a burden that I dreaded. I'd come home after a long day of teaching and crash out on the sofa, immovable until bedtime. My hobbies, which I'd previously been passionate about, fell by the wayside. I became irritable and rarely wanted to go any-where or do anything. I just wasn't any fun to be around. I started rethinking my career choice because if this was the way it was go-ing to be, then at some point I was going to come unhinged and run screaming for the parking lot.

My classroom, too, began to suffer. I didn't have the same energy. I wasn't as easygoing and affable and was unable to make the same connections with students as I had just a year or so before. I was less prepared and less sure of myself. I've always loved bringing humor into my classroom, more than anything, but that too was tapped out. I was spread as thin as rice paper and profoundly unhappy.

While in the midst of this day-after-day cycle of frustration and dissatisfaction, everything seemed to get on my nerves. In particular was when the principal or school district would spring something new on the staff or insist that we add this or that to my already overflowing plate. It would just about put me over the edge. I had no room, no buffer, and no patience to accept any-thing new or different with equanimity. I would smile and feign interest, while seething on the inside.

In an effort to please everyone and show that I was dedicated, my priorities got out of whack, and I wasn't good for anyone. I knew that if I were to stay in the profession I felt I was meant to be in, then I would have to make some changes.

At some point, out of desperation and the realization that I had nothing to lose, I began to say no. Slowly, tentatively at first, I said no. Then I said no some more. I resigned my position as an outdoor education trainer and began saying no to everything that pulled my time and attention away from my classroom and what was important to me in my life—like family, friends, and time to pursue interests outside of teaching. Although I didn't know it at the time, saying no was the first step to finding the 20 percent that made me happiest and most effective.

I said no to every committee I wasn't required to be on. I said no to GATE coordinator, homework club, and after school tutoring. I said no to coaching basketball, no to being in the school play, and no to going to the next reading conference. I also said no to distractions, wasting time, and boring meetings. (Again, those I didn't have to attend.) I said no to gossip, idle chitchat, complaining, and negativity. I even said no to things I enjoyed to a degree, but that ultimately added stress to my life.

"I'm sorry, I wish I could, but I'm really focused on my classroom."

"No, thank you. I appreciate you thinking of me, though."

"No, I don't think I'm the right person for that."

"No thanks!"

"Hey, good morning! Good to see you! We'll have to talk later. I've gotta run."

"No, I'm sorry. I don't have the time."

I learned that just being straight with people, but in a friendly way, was enough to end the conversation. It was enough to get out from under the two-ton refrigerator I had been carrying around on my back. It was enough to get my life back in balance.

Within a week, I was liberated. I was set free and empowered. It was a revelatory moment for me. I really didn't have to do it all, just what was important.

I also began saying no at home and in my personal life. If it wasn't essential or beneficial to those I cared about, then it was a no. I said no to perceived obligations and responsibilities and began zeroing in on what mattered most. I focused on just the essential few that supported my dreams for the future. The fog of depression lifted. I left work every day much earlier. I played golf and went to movies. I took my time at the gym. I started writing. I not only regained my love of teaching, but I became much better at it. To be good at anything, whether professionally or personally, takes a willingness, even eagerness, to say no.

Within two years of taking over at Apple, Steve Jobs reduced the number of products from 350 to 10, and said no hundreds, if not thousands of times to new proposals brought to him by his staff. Saying no became one of his core philosophies of business. Sheryl Sandberg, the Chief Operating Officer of Facebook, who is well known for her work-family balance, strictly maintains her priorities in a simple spiral notebook. She says no to busywork and wasteful, reactionary methods in favor of staying intently focused on her company's success.

When he was just starting out, Jimmy Fallon said no to paying work in commercials and television shows so he could focus on learning the skills he needed to fulfill his lifelong dream of being on *Saturday Night Live*. The Wright brothers rejected offers of partnerships and sponsorships to make their own decisions and pursue their passion for building the first reliable flying machine without distraction. Claude Monet had eight children and created thousands of paintings, drawings, and pastels, over 250 of water lilies alone. The author of *War & Peace*, Leo Tolstoy, had 13 children. No doubt both were experts at saying no. If you look at any great success, you'll find this simple act to be an overriding trait.

As for teaching, it's not only a secret to success, but it's a requirement. Saying no frees you to focus on those few things that add up to effective teaching—which we'll cover in subsequent chapters. It allows you to be at your energetic best for your students. It gives you the time you need to prepare and think and restore your spirit to its optimum level.

As a side benefit, you'll also find that you'll be able to cut your work hours. You'll be able to leave school earlier and rarely have to bring work home with you. Now, it's important to point out that saying no doesn't mean that you have to hide in your room and be anti-social. It doesn't mean that you have to give anyone the cold shoulder or be dishonest or say no to every committee or outside opportunity. You'll simply become more selective with your time and attention.

Saying no, however, does take a bit of discipline. It takes being purposeful in setting your priorities. It takes questioning nearly everything you do to determine whether it's part of the vital 20 percent that brings you closer to your happiness, or the trivial 80 percent that is muddling up your life. It takes examining how you spend your time at work each day.

Are you being productive or just busy? Are you talking about what you're going to do, or are you actually doing it? Are you rushing around and spinning your wheels, or are you methodically checking off items on your essential to-do list? Friendships with colleagues are important, but are the people you spend time with supportive and uplifting, or do they drag you down with negativity and gossip? Say yes to those few colleagues who have the same values and goals for their classroom as you do and politely pull away from those who don't.

Unless you reach a stage of desperation in your life like I did, saying no can feel uncomfortable at first. As teachers, we're givers and pleasers by nature. We want to feel like we're doing all we can to help our students, our school, and our community. We don't want to disappoint or offend anyone. We don't want to come off as rude and uncaring or selfish. It's normal to feel this way, but these fears are unfounded. We are far more effective when we have our priorities in order. We can only truly look outside ourselves and serve others when we have our act together, when we're not stressed, pressed for time, and wrapped up in our own drama.

The surprising truth is that most people will hold you in higher regard for saying no. They'll even start behaving differently around you. They'll become more sensitive of your time and appreciative of your advice and wisdom. Saying no is viewed as a virtue of strength, and is roundly admired and even envied. It's now been more than twenty years since I became so selective of my time, and I've had scores of people tell me how much they look up to the way I approach the job, protect the sanctity of my classroom, and yet have time for a life outside of work.

Saying no puts you in position to be the greatest benefit to your students, your family, and those you care most about. The more that is on your plate, the less effective you are, the less impressive you are, and the less helpful you are. Your energy and ability to concentrate are limited resources. You can either spread them thin and be unhappy and ineffective, or focus them on what's important and start making real headway on your goals and dreams for the future. Anyone—I don't care who you are, where you work, or how many children you have—can dramatically change their life by learning to tactfully decline.

The only rub is that it must be consistently maintained. If you're not careful, you can slowly yes your way back into stress and unhappiness. Just a couple of years ago, as my website began to grow, I had to relearn this lesson all over again. I knew consciously that I could reach a lot more people through my website and weekly newsletter than I ever could with individual teachers. But that didn't stop me from trying to answer every email question I received with a detailed and lengthy response.

Although I enjoy helping teachers one-on-one, I know that if I bite off more than I can chew, then the quality of my writing will suffer. I also said yes to interview requests. I wrote articles for other websites. I gave advice to other bloggers and offered particularly struggling teachers free personal coaching. These are all things I wanted to do, but they weren't the best use of my time. They pulled me away from my family, my contentment, and my ability to impact the greatest number of people. So I recommitted myself to saying no. I gave only one or two bits of advice instead of whole paragraphs. I promised to cover questions in future articles. I simply said that I was too busy.

You, too, may have to make difficult choices. You may have to say no to things you'd like to do, wish you could do, but that interfere with your ability to address your priorities. You may have to back away from friends that you care about, but who ultimately pull you away from what's important. You may have to reassess how you spend your time in support of your family. There is a big difference between your willingness to do anything for your children and a willingness to do what's best for them.

I know parents who drive their children all over town seven days a week for dance recitals, soccer practices, play dates, and more. They're wrung out and exhausted and don't even eat dinner as a family. They don't spend quality time together. I'm not saying that after school activities aren't beneficial, or important in their own right, but they aren't for everyone and certainly not every day of the week.

Maybe one or two days a week is better in the long run. Maybe saying no to the social pressure to play on a travel team or attend GATE summer school is the best thing you can do for your family. Maybe keeping up with the Joneses isn't in your family's best interest. In my experience, the happiest and most well-adjusted students spend the most time together with their family doing simple things: board games, backyard horseshoes, barbecues.

Regardless of whether you have five kids or none, among your priorities should include time to exercise, read a book, or take a walk in your neighborhood. Remember, if you're not at your best—if you're stressed, sleep deprived, unhealthy, and unable to recharge your batteries—then you're not going to be much good to anyone.

You must schedule time for yourself. Saying no happens to be a potent health elixir and stress reducer and the best and only sleep aid you'll ever need. It's about balancing your life. It's about going deeper in just a few areas, which is always infinitely more rewarding and successful than sampling a bit of everything. Surfers who put in the time to learn the intricacies of their sport experience joy every time they paddle out into the waves, whereas those who dabble usually get a mouth full of saltwater and a sore back.

Pare down your life to the essential few. Defend your time and energy. Say no to everything that draws you away from your peace of mind. And your life will change.

Just the other day an administrator pulled me into her office and asked me to sit down. She paced a bit. She sighed and shuffled a few papers on her desk before sitting down herself. She was clearly uncomfortable about what she was going to say and was gathering her thoughts.

Just when I started to get concerned, she began apologizing. She said she was sorry for taking up my time (I'd only been sitting there for a minute) and sorry for what she was about to ask me. She also said that it wouldn't hurt her feelings if I said no and that she would understand, but was wondering if maybe, just maybe, I'd be interested in attending . . . but before she could finish her sentence, I blurted out, "No, thank you." At that she rose from her seat, smiled, apologized again, and led me to the door.

Now, I don't recommend being so abrupt. Certainly people who don't know you may take offense. But saying no has been so important to my life that at times it rolls off the tongue a bit too quickly. The story also illustrates how deferentially people respond to those who know what they want. The truth is, there are only a few genuinely important things in life, and once you identify what they are, saying no becomes easy. It becomes something you no longer have to think about. Your internal understanding of what is right for you becomes so finely tuned that you'll rarely mull over decisions. You'll just know.

Saying no means saying yes to slowing down and smelling the roses. It means saying yes to quality time with your family and interests and causes that you love and care about. It means saying yes to freedom, flexibility, and focus. It means saying yes to effective teaching and yes to making an impact on your students that will last a lifetime. It means saying yes to a better, happier you.

Through the rainstorm came sanctuary
And I felt my spirit fly

-Seal, "Love's Divine"

Tidy

When I was a first-year teacher, a mentor of mine mentioned to me one day that she could tell how good a teacher was within a few seconds of walking into their empty classroom. It seemed implausible to me at the time, but I know now that a first impression of an after-hours classroom can be as accurate as spending an entire week observing its teacher.

In his 2005 book, *Blink*, Malcolm Gladwell recounts the story of Gianfranco Becchina. Becchina was an art dealer who approached the J. Paul Getty Museum in September of 1983 with a stunning sixth-century BC marble sculpture. Standing nearly seven feet tall, the statue depicted a young man with his arms at his side and one leg extended. While most similar pieces were badly damaged and often in fragments, this one was pristine. Becchina wanted almost $10 million for the sculpture and, although interested, museum curators were intent on doing their due diligence.

They took possession of the figure and spent months tracking down its provenance. They called in scientists to do detailed experimentation and analysis of the marble surface. They took core samples and X-rays and used the latest technology and equipment to determine its authenticity. After fourteen months of investigation, the Getty Museum agreed to purchase the Greek statue. It went on display for the first time in the fall of 1986.

But then a number of notable art historians and experts got a look at the sculpture. For reasons they couldn't quite put their finger on, they knew immediately that something was amiss. Years of experience told them that what they were looking at was a fake. Over time, and as the supporting documentation began to unravel, the museum concluded that it wasn't a rare antiquity after all, but a forgery just a year or two removed from a Roman workshop.

As it turns out, our intuition, shaped by years of study and experience, can be remarkably accurate. When my mentor made that offhanded comment to me now more than twenty years ago, little did I know how spot-on her observation was. In my current position of writing about teaching and classroom management, most of my time is spent breaking down my own "blink" moments and turning them into steps a reader can apply.

When I see a teacher making what I know to be a mistake, I then must determine the exact what and why of that mistake and conclude how to fix it. So while agreeing 100 percent with my former mentor, it's important to pinpoint what it is about those empty classrooms that are predictive of teaching success and how it can be replicated.

It was only after becoming a specialist teacher—that is, one who sees a new group of students each hour once or twice a week—that I was able to look deeper into the causes of teacher mistakes, as well as their successes. When I was a classroom teacher, my sole focus was on observing student behavior and how my class reacted to my strategies. I adjusted my approach over time until I felt confident in a system of classroom management that would bring peace and productivity to my classroom, regardless of the neighborhood I worked in or who showed up on my roster from year to year. Although I was able to help other teachers improve and eliminate misbehavior in their own classrooms, it wasn't until I became a specialist that I was able to really observe and analyze teacher behavior and understand the errors they made, as well as the implications of those errors.

I got to really know teachers and their tendencies and how students responded to them. What was especially instructive were my observations of each individual class when they arrived at my door for their weekly lesson. Students tend to take on the personality of their teacher. They reveal in their behavior, speaking, listening, maturity, and work habits precisely what is going on in their classrooms—both the good and the bad. It was fascinating to me and provided endless article topics for my books and blog.

I was also able to visit classrooms and see how students interacted with and reacted to various teachers, lesson styles, classroom management strategies, and personalities. I was able to observe teachers responding to misbehavior, teaching lessons, and guiding routines.

Although I didn't spend a great deal of time inside classrooms, whenever I did, one particular theme kept repeating itself. The best, happiest, and most confident teachers had classrooms that were notably lacking in clutter. In fact, for the most part, the more immaculate the classroom, the more effective the teacher was. Now, it's important to point out that I'm certain there are some anomalies. But they are few and far between. Personally, I've known only one especially effective teacher with a messy classroom.

Carol taught across the hall from me for several years and had dozens of boxes and old projects stacked above her cabinets. She also had experiments, knickknacks, and student work covering nearly every surface. Her desk, as well as many of her student's desks, was piled high with books, papers, and supplies. It gave me the heebie-jeebies just to walk into her room.

But she was an extraordinary personality who taught compelling and creative lessons. If she weren't a teacher, she would have been a great Broadway actress. She sang and danced and playacted through much of the school day. Her remarkable presence allowed her to bypass many of the hallmarks of successful teaching. For the rest of us, though, maintaining a clutter-free learning environment is critical to our success. The reasons are many, but the most obvious is the effect messiness and disorder has on children.

In a 2006 study conducted at the University of Sussex, researchers discovered a clear link between cleanliness and good behavior. It makes sense. When the visual stimuli is chaotic, children tend to behave chaotically. Clutter causes stress and interferes with their sense of safety and well being. It sends the message that no one cares. According to the American Academy of Pediatrics, a messy home is a greater predictor of bad behavior than even parenting style. A cluttered classroom also affects listening and focus. *The Journal of Neuroscience* published a study in 2011 that concluded that too many varied objects in a child's field of vision negatively affects their ability to concentrate. It slows learning, limits their ability to process information, and increases nervousness and irritability.

In my own observations, the overriding behavior I see associated with clutter is excitability. Students appear to be agitated and unable to sit still. There is a hum of tension you can feel the moment you step into the room. Teachers grow so accustomed to this feeling that they either don't notice it anymore or assume that it's just the nature of teaching. It's not. The presence of tension is a sign that learning is suffering and students are unhappy. Those who may have a proclivity to misbehave or who have trouble focusing tend to struggle the most. Often, the most effective thing you can do for them is clean up the learning environment.

Clutter also deeply affects the teacher and their ability to focus on their job and their students. Overflowing cabinets, boxes piled in corners, art projects yellowing on the walls, papers and materials stacked on tables, and backpacks lying on the floor all compete for the teacher's attention. It's like having an additional ten students in your classroom. The brain can't take it all in. It can't weed it all out. The bombardment of stimuli stresses the system and won't allow you to be your best, most inspirational self for your students. It causes you to feel as if you're never in control, which then shows in your teaching.

On a recent Monday morning, I entered a friend's classroom to discuss the college basketball games that took place over the weekend. We usually spend a few minutes every Monday recounting how well or how poorly our alma maters performed. His classroom is spotless, almost spartan in its appearance. It looks like a law library minus the rows of books. He had his feet up on his empty desk and was reading from the short story he planned to introduce that day to his students. He was relaxed if not a bit tired, but was in no particular hurry. Our conversation ran longer than normal and his students began entering the classroom. He said little to them as they hung their backpacks neatly on individual hooks that lined the back wall and began working on an independent activity he had written on the whiteboard. They, too, were relaxed. They moved purposefully and appeared comfortable but focused on the task at hand.

I waved goodbye, and as I walked past the classroom next door, the difference was striking. The students were shouting and pushing and slamming their things onto their desks. It looked like a beehive short on nectar. The teacher, already stressed out, was yelling over the din to try and reel them in. Now, there are many variables that account for an ill-behaved classroom, but for this particular teacher, foremost among them was that every day the students had to walk into a visually chaotic environment. The impact on the senses was of disarray and disorder. Here it was Monday morning and the students were already agitated and primed to misbehave. The teacher was behind the eight ball from the second the morning bell rang.

Most teachers believe they're doing pretty well in this area, that although they can improve, their classroom certainly isn't a mess. But here's the thing: The most effective teachers are fanatical in their commitment to neatness. Not only is the visual effect of entering their classroom calming and comforting, but even the contents of the closed cabinets and desk drawers are organized and easily accessible. This isn't simply a reflection of personal style or preference. Maintaining a pin-neat classroom will directly, and often dramatically, improve *any* teacher's ability to focus. It also saves time, lowers stress, soothes frayed and tattered nerves, and fills with renewed confidence.

So why doesn't everyone tidy and organize their classroom? Well, one reason is that it often takes actually doing it to realize what an amazing effect it has. Teachers are shocked at how much more relaxed and in control they feel. They're taken aback by the impact it has on their students and how seemingly every adult who enters has a comment about the look and feel of their classroom. There is a sense of respect and reverence that reflects sky-high expectations and prompts everyone in its presence to up their game.

But it does take some initial work. In most cases, it takes throwing out or donating a mountain of unused and outdated supplies and resources. It can take an entire day or two to whip most classrooms into shape. There are also some notable psychological barriers that can keep teachers from jumping in and getting to work.

In an article for *The Atlantic*, Bourree Lam describes three hurdles that keep people from clearing the physical clutter from their life. They are based on some key economic concepts and are particularly applicable to teachers struggling to get rid of excess accumulation.

The first hurdle is referred to as the sunk cost fallacy. The way it works is that if you or someone else has put time or money into something, it feels like a waste not to use it. So, for example, say you spent six dollars and an hour of your time watching a pay-per-view movie you don't like. Because you've invested resources that you can never get back, you're likely to finish watching that movie. It may be irrational not to just cut your losses and shut it off, but you sit through it anyway.

This sunk cost behavior is very common and accounts for why teachers have a tendency to hang on to so much stuff. The idea that you or your school purchased or created something for your students, even if it was years ago and no longer viable, makes it difficult to get rid of. Although you may have no intention of using it, and it's providing no benefit whatsoever, it feels wrong to throw it away.

I've personally witnessed teachers agonize over materials that were no longer even part of the curriculum. They were hanging on to things passed down to them from teachers long ago retired. I've found that one of the best ways to combat this internal struggle is to take anything that was purchased by the school to the resource teacher, custodian, vice-principal, or whoever is in charge of disseminating teaching materials to the staff. Simply tell them that you're no longer using it. Leave it to them to decide whether to ship it back to the school district, donate it, throw it away, or pass it along to someone who may use it. This is part of their job, and it's important that you take advantage of it. In this way, you can relieve yourself of the burden of feeling like you're wasting a resource, while at the same time clearing more space in your classroom. You'll find that many items fall into this category.

The second hurdle that dissuades teachers from decluttering is called the status quo bias. This refers to the tendency to keep something because you can't think of a good reason to get rid of it. You get so used to that old box of art project ideas being part of your classroom that you hang on to it. In one sense, it's comforting to know that you have it just in case. But by hanging on to things for a rainy day, we don't realize the burden they exert on our emotional well-being. We don't realize how they muddle our thinking and add stress to our lives. It's only after we get rid of them that we feel a weight has been lifted.

Marie Kondo, the author of *The Life-Changing Magic of Tidying Up*, stresses that the best way to handle items that fall into this category is to decide straight away to throw them out unless you have a compelling reason to keep them. By turning the status quo bias mindset on its head, and looking at it from the opposite direction, you'll find it much easier to rid yourself of the excess that is weighing you down. This creates a new status quo for yourself. That is, when in doubt, get rid of it.

The third and final hurdle to clearing out clutter is called the folly of prediction. People tend to hang on to things they will never use because they believe that maybe, someday in the future, they might need them. But research has shown that people are poor predictors of the future. Most teachers will never use two-thirds or more of what is taking up space in their classroom, which is another example of the 80/20 rule at work.

Part of what is driving their inaccurate predictions is that people, in general, assign more value to things that belong to them. Study after study has proven this to be true. To break this pattern of thinking, Kondo recommends focusing on what to keep rather than what to get rid of. Ask yourself not only whether you're going to really use the item again, but also whether it's something that will positively benefit you, your students, or your curriculum. If not, getting rid of it is a slam-dunk. In my many years of teaching with an extremely limited amount of materials, I can honestly say that I've never regretted getting rid of anything. I also know that in a pinch I can borrow what I need from a colleague, as they sometimes do from me.

Giving your classroom a makeover is best done in one fell swoop. Choose a Saturday or, if you're reading this over the summer, a day that affords you a few hours of uninterrupted work. Although it's tempting to recruit a family member for help, you'll find it easier to make decisions while you're alone. Ask your spouse or a friend to meet you later in the day to help you haul out the discarded materials. Start with your desk and work your way out to the rest of the room. By taking care of the most personal items first, you'll be empowered to tackle the rest with more confidence.

Try not to think too hard before making decisions. Go with your first instinct. If it isn't clearly something you want to keep, then either place it in the center of your room—if it's something others may find valuable—or put it in one of the several heavy-duty trash bags you brought with you. If it's the former, keep two separate piles—one for school-bought items you'll take to your contact person and one for things you've purchased and will donate yourself or offer to other teachers. Knowing that others may use what would otherwise collect dust makes the process easier. But the truth is, once you get going, it will feel so good, and you'll be so energized, that knowing what to keep will become more and more obvious.

After paring your resources down to the essentials, turn your attention to the appearance of your classroom. For most teachers, this requires a considerable change in thinking. It's common to want to make your classroom look inviting. But adding sofas, bean bag chairs, floor lamps, and excessive decorative items translates to clutter. Your classroom should reflect the purposefulness, attention to detail, and impeccable behavior you expect from your students. Any object or item that can be put away should be put away. In the absence of students, your room should look simple, plain, even austere. Think in terms of an exhibition room of a museum rather than your corner Starbucks.

The more cubic space you can free up in your classroom, the more your students will thrive. The physical environment should be a drumbeat message looping day after day that excellence is expected. Extreme order supports and even enhances your emphasis on active listening and politeness. It calms and focuses. It pleases the eye and the heart.

This doesn't mean that you shouldn't have colorful posters or art projects adorning the walls or science projects on the windowsill. It means that they'll be arranged neatly and sharply and never left to curl or fade. Remember, though, it isn't the physical environment that adds life to your classroom. It's you. It's your personality. It's your passion and humor. It's your happy and productive students.

Benjamin Franklin once said that for every minute spent organizing, an hour is earned. Not only is this a truism for time management, but it's so much more. It might be the best decision you ever make as a teacher.

Clearing out the clutter and tidying up your classroom will have a profound effect, regardless of where you are in your career. The release of stress and the sense of control you'll feel are worth the few hours spent sifting through boxes and separating the useful from the useless. And the effect is immediate. A weight you never knew existed will slide off your shoulders. You'll smile and keep on smiling. You'll become a different teacher. You'll feel like you can do anything.

The biggest payoff, however, is when your students first walk through your door on Monday morning. They'll tiptoe in, wide-eyed and surprised. They'll be noticeably calmer and appear to have more respect for you, for each other, and for their learning. They'll breathe easier and settle into their seats more contented than they've been since the first day of school. And when you open your mouth to speak, they'll listen. Because your words will finally match what they see all around them.

We gotta keep the fire burning
Come on and dream baby dream

-Bruce Springsteen, "Dream Baby Dream"

Inspire

It wasn't long after I began my teaching career that I started questioning the efficacy of external rewards and incentives. It was my first year of teaching and I had been using the old Lee Canter strategy of placing gumballs in a large jar whenever my class did anything well, like entering the classroom, transitioning, or performing routines and procedures as I taught them.

The "ting" each gumball made when striking the bottom of the glass was an auditory signal that they had done something correctly. My students seemed to respond to it, especially after I revealed that when the jar was full, we'd celebrate with a party. I stuck with the strategy per the instructions I was given during the teacher training program I'd recently graduated from. But despite this being a "proven" strategy many other teachers were using, it felt strange to me. It seemed demeaning to students. I felt like one of those panda trainers at the zoo who offer honey water in return for compliant behavior. But I stuck with it because it seemed to work—at least for awhile.

I've always been an observer of human behavior. More than a few times as a child I had to apologize for staring in class. It made me feel like a creep, but I was just curious. I wanted to know why people behaved the way they did and how outside forces could mold and shape that behavior. That curiosity led me to study psychology in college and become a teacher. I was determined that first year in the classroom—and every year since—to test any and every method I used. I watched and took notes and adjusted my teaching until I felt confident in a strategy or approach that worked over time and with a great majority of students.

I also sought methods that had the best interest of students and their long-term success at heart. So as I was dropping gumballs in that big glass jar those first few weeks into my teaching career, I was keeping track of how students behaved in response. They seemed excited about it at first, but before long, it began to lose its influence. The novelty had worn off and the promise of a party seemed too far in the distance to keep them motivated.

I, too, was bored by the strategy. So on a whim one day I started throwing the gumballs in the jar from about five feet away. Before I'd make my toss, a few students would raise their hands over their head, and as the gumball would fall into the jar, they would bring their hands down and yell, "whoosh!" One of them had seen this on television while watching basketball. I thought it was funny, and so I encouraged everyone to join in. Soon, the whole class would stand with their hands up before I'd shoot.

I then started stepping back a few more feet and offering that if I made it, I'd put an additional gumball in the jar. This made the moment more exciting, and my students couldn't wait for the couple of times during the day when we'd take a break and shoot gumballs.

By this time it began dawning on me that it wasn't the reward that kept them interested and motivated to follow my routines and directions, but rather it was the fun we were having together. It was the moment that mattered, not the carrot. I eventually dropped the gumball idea altogether, but not before taking the fun to the next level. As interest waned yet again, I began shooting once a week from the other side of the room. I told the students that if I made it, which seemed to me an impossibility, we'd have an automatic party.

Those Friday afternoons became not-miss events. If any student had to be pulled for speech, resource, or other programs, they would beg me to wait until they returned before I would shoot. As I would position myself in the back of the room, they would stand, hold their hands high, and jump up and down. Teachers and students in other classrooms would ask me what we were doing and what all the racket was about. The principal and other staff members and parents would come in to watch.

One day the unthinkable happened and one of those little gumballs dropped into the jar from about thirty-five feet away. It rattled around a bit, bounced up above the rim, and then fell in. The class erupted. I dropped to my knees like a tennis player who had just won Wimbledon. We danced and high-fived for several minutes.

Over the next couple of years I experimented with prize boxes, token economies, and individual rewards. I gave out stickers and gummy bears and holiday pencils. I tried out behavior contracts and no-homework passes. I "caught students being good" and handed out monthly awards. I tried every reward system in one incarnation or the other that are still popular today. Over time and one by one I eliminated them all from my teaching. I concluded that not only were they a huge pain in the backside, and ineffective over time, but they were far less powerful than cultivating a classroom culture that encourages intrinsic motivation.

After 25 years of teaching, I now believe more strongly than ever that offering rewards in exchange for good behavior is harmful to students and makes creating a well-behaved classroom much, much harder. A learning environment that allows intrinsic rewards to flourish, on the other hand, is a lot more effective, a lot more fun, and remarkably less stressful.

Although throwing out external rewards swims against the tide of most modern day school districts, there is a mountain of research reaching back as far as the 1940s supporting its wisdom. Daniel Pink's book, *Drive*, in particular, lays out the evidence in a most convincing way and includes a summation of the most important studies in the field.

Many school districts around the country, however, continue to beat the drum of prizes, trinkets, and awards in exchange for good behavior and performance. They even appear to be becoming more popular, as evidenced by the growing number of schools that are adopting token economies and other rewards-based behavior programs. If you've attended a training, then you've no doubt heard the claims that these programs are research-based.

And this is true. But what they don't tell you is what that research actually says.

Studies have proven that rewards can indeed motivate people to do what you want them to do, but they have serious drawbacks and limitations. The most critical of which is that they weaken intrinsic motivation—if not eliminate it altogether. By offering students points or prizes for good behavior or attentiveness, you're communicating to them that being conscientious, respectful, and kind is *work* deserving of payment. You're putting a price tag on what is inherently rewarding, effectively snuffing out the intrinsic value of doing the right thing.

The result is that in the long run you get the opposite of the intended effect. Rewards can even embolden unethical behavior like cheating and cutting corners. They also decrease in effectiveness over time, meaning that you have to continually up the ante or your students will grow bored and disinterested.

For example, let's say you offer a certain number of tokens or points in exchange for politely working and completing a group project. You may very well encourage your students to get it done, but you take the intrinsic joy out of it. They'll believe they're doing it just to receive the prize at the end. The fun of working together and creating something unique and special falls by the wayside. For future projects, you make them even less motivated unless you keep paying them at a higher and higher rate. And because you've removed its intrinsic value, they're unlikely to become engaged in the project. They're unlikely to reach that *flow* state where they become lost in their work, where the activity becomes worth doing simply for the enjoyment and challenge it brings.

The work, then, suffers and the project becomes just another hoop to jump through. They become bored and desirous of something real and more meaningful—even if it's misbehavior. In my observations of students, when they're offered rewards for their work, they may smile and even enjoy the prize, but deep down they're often profoundly disappointed, especially those who love learning to begin with. A reward cheapens their effort. If you observe closely, some students will even look at you pleadingly, as if to say, "Please don't buy my joy. It's not for sale."

Whether it's trying to encourage students to love school, engage in better group conversations, or treat each other with more respect, if it's something that has intrinsic value, then you should never, ever attach rewards to it. Doing so will sabotage those efforts. It will cause students to *lose* interest. It will transform what is naturally alluring and rewarding into drudgery.

The only time rewards may be appropriate in school is if you're asking students to perform a mechanical, left-brain task like helping you staple papers or put away library books. If it doesn't have intrinsic value to begin with, then rewarding with a sticker or an eraser is harmless and may indeed motivate students to volunteer for and complete the task. But for anything meaningful that you want to encourage, the worst thing you can do is offer rewards. The body of research clearly shows them to be antithetical to the kind of passionate, on fire for learning environment in which kids thrive.

Teachers who remove "do this and get that" rewards from their classroom also find that it removes a giant burden from their shoulders. They feel liberated from the constant need to manipulate students into doing what they ask. They're free from having to think about what rewards to buy and how to use them. They no longer have to keep track of points or worry about who should get what and when. They no longer have to hear students complaining about why they didn't get this reward or that one. They no longer have to participate in something that deep down they never really felt good about.

Removing rewards will also transform your teaching. It will shift your focus from trying to light a fire under individual students to creating a learning environment every student will appreciate and enjoy being part of. Your personality, charisma, and passion for teaching will step to the forefront. You'll become more dynamic and inspirational. Your students will be drawn to you and want to get to know you better. You'll also be far more at ease walking into your classroom.

These are natural consequences of a reward-free classroom. They are byproducts that will result in your students becoming more intrinsically motivated. If you do nothing else, you'll be happier and more effective by refusing to pay for attentiveness, good work habits, and expected behavior. However, there is one thing you can do to maximize the effect. There is one thing that will transform your students into the independent, well-behaved class you've always wanted.

At 7:51 in the morning on January 12, 2007, Joshua Bell walked into the L'Enfant Plaza Metro station in Washington, D.C., pulled out a violin, and started playing. For the next 43 minutes, just over 1,000 people passed by on their way to and from the trains that circle and crisscross the city. A few tossed a dollar or two into the instrument case at his feet, but most hurried past on their way to work without a second glance. Only seven people stopped to listen for longer than a minute, which isn't unusual for the many musicians that set up shop in train stations and bus depots around the area.

But Bell isn't just another musician. He is one of the greatest violinists of his generation. His virtuoso performances sell out everywhere from Carnegie Hall to the Philharmonie de Paris. He combines technical wizardry with passion and tasteful interpretation to create magical renditions of some of the finest pieces of music ever written. That morning in January, Bell began his performance with Bach's "Chaconne," a notoriously difficult but gorgeous piece lasting nearly fifteen minutes. In order, he then played Schubert's "Ava Maria," Ponce's "Estrellita," a short piece by Jules Massenet, a Bach gavotte (music intended for a dance of the same name), and finished with a reprise of "Chaconne."

The 39-year-old Bell, dressed in a t-shirt and jeans and wearing a baseball cap, was in the L'Enfant station that day as part of an experiment in context. *The Washington Post* was curious to see if beauty would inevitably transcend the commonplace. Would people recognize a great work of art in a place they least expected to find it? As the minutes rolled by, and as Bell performed one masterpiece after another, the answer became, for the most part, no. But that doesn't mean that the experiment wasn't fascinating.

As described by *The Washington Post* writer Gene Weingarten, every child who walked by, pulled along by a parent, turned and stared at Bell from the moment they entered the station lobby. Those few people who stopped to listen, often did so after first walking by. One person, Stacy Furukawa, recognized Bell toward the end of his performance. She settled in just 10 feet away to witness the final strokes of his bow. John David Mortensen leaned against a wall for the few minutes he had before commuting to work because he said that, although he wasn't a fan of classical music, the sound coming from the guy in the New York Mets hat made him feel at peace. Mortensen's keen ear overcame the lack of context. The person who stayed the longest was John Picarello.

Picarello didn't recognize Bell, but was so moved by the caliber of the music that he walked some distance away so as not to intrude on Bell's space. He mentioned being baffled that others didn't notice or understand the magnitude of what they were hearing. But John Picarello was a classical music aficionado. He studied violin as a child and even considered becoming a concert musician. Upon hearing Bell, he knew what he was hearing was the work of a genius. He could appreciate it and was moved by it because he had spent a lifetime listening to classical music. He didn't need context.

If the thousand or so commuters who ignored Bell that day were handed $200 tickets and a limousine ride to The Kennedy Center, with its seven crystal chandeliers and acoustical canopy, to watch Bell on stage in front of an orchestra, then their reactions to his performance would have likely been very much like Picarello's. The more appropriate context would have placed them in a frame of mind to appreciate Bell's artistry.

But with Bell standing next to a trash can in an everyday metro station, they needed someone to point out why what they were hearing was worth listening to. They needed someone with the passion and enthusiasm for classical music like Picarello to *teach* them, to provide the context the environment wasn't able to deliver. Only then would they have been compelled to stop and take in the performance. Only then could they begin a journey into their own love of classical music.

So often our students stroll by lessons like commuters on their way to work, their minds and hearts far away from the topic and groping for a connection. They're bored and antsy and primed to misbehave. To then offer a reward to them for their attention is not only lazy teaching, but it pushes the intrinsic value of learning even further away. It snuffs out the *flow* experience and makes them less interested in what you have to say.

As teachers, our primary job is to provide context, to bring depth and meaning and vivacity to our lessons. It's to point out what is interesting, lovely, tragic, beautiful, heartbreaking, and otherwise noteworthy about our topic and then to fill in the backstory, the history, and the details that make it worth learning.

If Joshua Bell had paid every person who walked by him that day 20 dollars to stop and listen, he would have had quite a crowd. But by paying them he also would have turned what was a once-in-a-lifetime experience into an obligation. It's the same with your students. When you pay them via rewards you ruin the joy of learning for its own sake. You sabotage your efforts to make your classroom a place they look forward to. But by eschewing rewards and focusing instead on immersing students into the subject matter, you transform them into self-motivated learners.

This enlivened approach to education simplifies teaching to its essential core. It allows you to do the job you've always wanted to do and in the way you always dreamed of doing it. It frees you to teach with passion to an audience captivated by the remarkable connections, stories, and fascinations that are wired to your subject. It puts you smack dab in the middle of that Washington, D.C. metro station with the ability to say, "Stop! This is Joshua Bell. What you're hearing is divine and here's why." It turns your classroom into an engrossing experience from opening bell to dismissal.

This doesn't mean that you can never have class parties. It doesn't mean you can never pass out stickers or head out to recess early or hold a Friday afternoon dance contest. It just means that you're going to include everyone and that you're not going to connect these experiences to any particular behavior. You'll do them if you wish simply because it helps make your classroom more fun and rewarding in its own right. Your humor and personality, too, add to the experience and cause your students to arrive at your classroom door each day happy and expectant.

It is this combination of contextualized lessons—which we'll learn how to create and present in the coming chapters—and a joyful, lively classroom that cause students to become intrinsically motivated. It is this combination that gets stronger over time, that delivers a group of students on the last day of school that is far different than the one that began the school year. It is this combination that results in a love of school for them and a love of teaching for you.

I've met few teachers who haven't grown to dislike using rewards intensely. Not only are they a constant headache, but they leave teachers feeling deceitful and manipulative. They leave them exhausted and wishing there were another way.

Rewarding students in exchange for good behavior and academic performance is a short-term fix that rips the heart and soul out of teaching. It makes it a cold transaction, a straight bribe in return for a *show* of attentiveness. After all, it isn't real. In the presence of rewards, there is no pure love of learning. There is no learning for its own sake. There is no absorption in the educational experience. It's been choked out by a promise of free time, wash-off tattoos, and rubber wristbands.

Throwing it all out can be scary, to be sure. To stand in front of your students for the first time with nothing more than an idea and a story can be daunting. But it's also exhilarating. It's career transforming. It's an act of faith that places into your hands a tiny seed from which inspiration grows.

The minute you do away with all the rewards and prize boxes and tokens and such, the act of teaching steps onto center stage. Every day we use the magic of context to dress our students up in tuxedos and sparkling dresses. We stroll the beautiful lobby and point out the richly appointed staircases and gold leaf ornamentation. We lead them down the aisle of the storied theater to their seats near the front of the vast stage.

And then the curtain opens . . .

"It sounds obvious, but I wonder how many people, whatever their medium, appreciate the gift of improvisation."

-Twyla Tharp, author of *The Creative Habit*

"Studying improvisation literally changed my life."

-Tina Fey

Improvise

On October 24th, 1911 Robert Falcon Scott and his crew of adventurers left Cape Evans, Antarctica, located along the edge of the continent, and headed for the southern most point on Earth. They were endeavoring to be the first human beings to reach the South Pole.

After weeks of arduous travel, the party was heartened when on January 9th, 1912 they passed the previous record of "farthest south" held by polar legend Ernest Shackleton. Just seven days later, however, and a mere 15 miles from their goal, they spotted a black flag in the distance. They reached the pole the next day only to confirm their disappointment: A Norwegian explorer named Roald Amundsen, who had also been the first to reach the North Pole, had beaten them to it. Demoralized, they snapped a few photographs and then turned for home. Over the next two months, battling frostbite, fatigue, and starvation, all five members of the expedition perished in their tents just 11 miles from safety. It was a tragic end to a heroic effort.

In the century since, countless researchers have pored over records and correspondence searching for answers to why Scott and his party succumbed to the harsh and bitter conditions while Amundsen's team was able to complete the journey and return home safely and in relatively good health. Dozens of books and hundreds of articles have been written on the topic, and while acknowledging a remarkable run of bad luck, most point the finger at Scott himself. He made countless errors including his choice of teammates and reliance on unproven technology.

Many cite Scott as a dramatic example of what can happen when you fail to plan. But Scott didn't fail to plan. He planned and arranged for the expedition for years and had extensive polar experience. It just didn't work. He underestimated the importance of having experts in equipment and navigation on his crew. He emphasized the scientific aspects of the journey and collected samples that slowed their progress. Most of all, he relied too heavily on human power and endurance to haul supplies rather than sled dogs. His planning didn't match the unique challenges of the task.

Amundsen, on the other hand, had the right prescription for the job. His crew consisted of expert skiers rather than scientists, who were trained in navigation and equipment maintenance. He relied entirely on sled dogs from start to finish. Most importantly, Amundsen's expedition had the one and only goal of reaching the South Pole and returning alive. His focus was singular and thus undistracted from his team's moment-to-moment needs of survival.

Like Robert Falcon Scott's ill-fated preparations, today's educational leaders, as well as many administrators, are preparing teachers for failure. The *amount* of time spent training isn't the problem, as evidenced by the countless time-consuming professional development meetings that pull teachers away from their class-rooms. The problem is the focus of all that work. The problem is that it leaves teachers lost when they have to actually stand in front of their students to communicate, motivate, and inspire.

The thrust of nearly all teacher development these days is curriculum implementation, with the occasional teaching strat-egy thrown in. Which is all fine and good, but what teachers ac-tually need to know in these areas can be learned in a fraction of the time. Curriculum trainers and experts will take two hours to describe, through a haze of edu-speak, acronyms, and buzz-words, what can be summed up in a few sentences. They make what should be—and is—simple and straightforward into a web of complexity. They major in minor things, focusing on a small area of education at the expense of the one thing that will most improve teaching. They ignore the one and only thing you need to focus on in order to become an exceptional teacher, the one thing that will get your students to sit up, lean in, and be eager to learn.

On August 30th, 2015 I tuned into ESPN's telecast of *Sunday Night Baseball* (SNB), which is their national showcase they promote heavily throughout the week. The Dodgers were playing the Cubs, and as it turned out, it was a remarkable game. Jake Arrieta, Chicago's starting pitcher, threw a no-hitter. It was a tense, nail-biting affair. But it was notable for more than just the action on the field.

Throughout most of the summer the SNB broadcast team consisted of John Kruk, Curt Schilling, and Dan Schulman. Schulman provided play-by-play duties and Kruk and Schilling handled color commentary. On this particular night, however, there was a change in the broadcast booth. Earlier in the week Curt Schilling was suspended by ESPN for insensitive comments he made on Twitter, and former Olympic gold medal-winning softball player Jessica Mendoza was filling in.

Within just a few minutes of plopping down in front of the television, it was clear to me that although it was her first time on SNB, Mendoza was special. I didn't know who she was at the time, but I was immediately struck by her extensive knowledge of the game and relaxed communication skills. The detail with which she described why Arrieta was so successful, from how he kept the Dodger hitters off balance to his pitch selection to the spin and location of his curveball, was remarkable. It drove me deeper into the game. She relied on fascinating behind-the-scenes nitty-gritty to bring the drama of the moment into my living room. She had an in-depth knowledge of the history of the sport and knew the backgrounds of the participants and their past successes and failures. She told stories and painted word images.

She not only belonged in the booth with the two seasoned professionals, but she was undoubtedly the star. As it turns out, I wasn't the only one who noticed. The response to her work, from media critics and casual fans alike, was overwhelming. In one evening, she cemented herself as part of ESPN's baseball coverage for the rest of the season.

What struck me most beyond her insight was her ability to keep her composure. Here she was working with ESPN's flagship team on national television while a near-perfect game was being thrown on the field below. Yet, she appeared as comfortable as if she were sitting on the sofa across from me. She didn't ramble on, speak too quickly, or bring any extra attention to herself, as so many commentators do. She communicated smoothly and naturally and in a way that meshed well with the other two announcers.

Her facts and anecdotes only added to the viewer's enjoyment and immersion in the events happening on the field. The game was brighter and more interesting because of her presence.

So how did she do it—under the bright lights, inexperienced, and being the very first female ESPN baseball commentator? Moreover, it turns out that it was only her second time announcing a Major League Baseball game *ever*. It seems impossible. But as it turns out, she had an advantage—an advantage that made her appear so relaxed, so in control, and so authentic. It's an advantage utilized by great speakers, politicians, actors, and salespeople, whose very success depends on their ability to draw people in and capture their attention. It's a secret of sorts few teachers outside of the drama department have ever heard of, but one that can change everything.

Before she stepped into the booth that warm Sunday night, Jessica spent days preparing for the game. She studied statistics. She interviewed players and coaches. She watched video footage of the two starting pitchers and learned their unique throwing motions and tendencies. She pored over local newspapers of both teams and scoured the internet for personal interest stories. She asked questions and mined for information. She dug deep. She acquired the knowledge needed to be interesting to the viewer. When asked about her preparation process, Mendoza remarked that she goes into a game with "ten hours at least of information to talk about."

Although she may have had lessons or taken classes in television broadcasting, and she may very well brush up on her camera skills in the off-season, it isn't the focus of her preparation. Her focus is on content. Her focus is on knowing so much about her subject that she can relax and tell stories, provide context, and point out insider details to the viewer. She is compelling and charismatic because she knows her stuff.

It's the same with effective teaching. Curriculum and teaching methods are important, to be sure. You need to know what to teach and how you're expected to deliver it to your students. But this knowledge alone has little to do with being a good teacher. It has little to do with motivating and inspiring students.

School districts pour millions of dollars into training teachers how to implement curriculum, how to conduct guided reading groups, how to use manipulatives to teach math, and so on. But this isn't what inspires students to learn. You do. It's the teacher that makes the difference. It's your personality and charisma and ability to capture and keep attention that determines how effective you'll be. In fact, all that training actually constricts great teaching. It leaves teachers inflexible, mechanical, and devoid of passion.

To be the teacher you've always wanted to be, the kind students love and are motivated by, you need to be an expert in your subject matter. You need to be an expert of 18th century literature or the American Revolution or geometry or whatever subject you stand or sit in front of your students to teach. It is content knowledge that allows you to share the little-known histories, backgrounds, and anecdotes that make your subject come to life.

Deep knowledge of content provides a wellspring of avenues to add color, texture, and context for your students. Paul Revere's ride takes on a whole new meaning when you're able to fill in the backstory, uncover the drama, and place your students in the saddle of his borrowed horse as he galloped to Lexington that night. Content knowledge is the one thing. It is the secret to great teaching because it provides the minutia that students find fascinating.

It also frees you to do something that at first glance may seem reckless, but is the key to having the kind of magnetic personality that draws students in.

The Second City of Chicago is the most famous improvisational comedy school in the world. With alumni like Tina Fey, Steve Carell, John Belushi, Bill Murray, Amy Poehler, and many others, it's no wonder aspiring comedians and actors flock to its North Side location. If you've ever been to a performance, then you've been amazed at their ability to create hilarity out of thin air. They can take a prop, location, or suggestion from the audience and build a comedic story that entertains and mesmerizes the audience. We often assume that this ability takes a level of genius or wittiness that isn't accessible to the rest of us. We assume that even the performers at our local improv theater were born with a special gift. When we see Wayne Brady or Colin Mochrie from *Whose Line Is It Anyway?* make up a song or dance or act out a scene on the spot, we think that there is no way we could do that.

And while the famous performers mentioned above are certainly gifted, as it turns out we all have access to the same genius. Second City, after all, is a school. It teaches principles of improvisation that enable *anyone* to tap into the natural wisdom they have inside. They are the same principles that Jessica Mendoza relied on when she stepped into the announcer's booth for the first time. They are the same principles you can use to become similarly captivating to your students.

Jessica Mendoza used her exhaustive knowledge of baseball to draw the audience into the most fascinating aspects of the game. She made it interesting even to those who find it boring by delving deeper and by making connections to everyday life. Although she may have had notes, she made us care about what was happening on the field by speaking off the top of her head. She improvised her way through all nine innings.

One of the most striking things about watching *Whose Line Is It Anyway?* is how intellectually well-rounded the performers are. They're never stumped or lacking anything to say because they're able to draw on their knowledge of history, politics, music, and popular culture. Knowing your content is the first step to being interesting. It's the first step to freeing the natural wisdom and charisma you have inside. But content alone isn't enough.

As I write this, the candidates for US president are vying for position and trying to climb their way up in the polls. One particular candidate is known for his extensive knowledge and experience in domestic affairs, the economy, foreign trade, and other matters critical for the job. But when he speaks he sounds practiced. He appears stiff and inauthentic. In one-on-one interviews he lacks emotional connection, and it's hurting him in the polls. This candidate has the knowledge, but not the improvisational skills to deliver it in a convincing way.

There are three principles of improvisation as they apply to teaching that will give you a quality and presence that all great teachers share. Together, they make up a way of communicating that educational experts have been trying and failing for decades to put their finger on.

The first principle is simple, but very, very powerful. The way it works is that before stepping in front of your students to begin any lesson or activity, you have to clear your mind of any and all thoughts of how you want to express yourself. You have to let go of the script in your head. You have to let go of trying to be clever. You have to let go of thinking ahead or thinking up what you want to say. Instead, you must be in the moment—ready, nimble, and open to whatever may come. This doesn't mean that you'll be un-prepared. You'll still be aware of your objective and how you want your students to prove that objective. You'll still have a visualization of the stories or examples you want to use. You'll still know how much time you need for each segment of your lesson. But otherwise, you will simply trust your natural wisdom.

All great performers do this. They brush aside their mental clutter before stepping on stage, walking to the plate, or setting brush to canvas. They know that if their thoughts are on anything but what is immediately in front of them, then their work will suffer. It's an exercise in getting into *flow*. When you lock into the present moment, what you need to do and say to best communicate your objectives becomes obvious. It becomes clearer than you've ever experienced before. You'll be both amazed and surprised at the wisdom that comes out of your mouth, and how much more engaged and attentive your students will be.

When we think ahead, we become clumsy and robotic. We have only the foggiest picture of the here and now, completely missing the motivational needs of our students. Thinking ahead rather than being fully in the present renders you ineffective and unaware. Freeing your mind of clutter, on the other hand, sharpens the picture, frees your personality, and allows your innate communication skills to shine. We suddenly become poised, empathetic, and attuned to the world around us. We make instant connections and associations. We become our best and most authentic selves.

The second principle is to not try too hard. In her fantastic book, *Improv Wisdom*, Patricia Ryan Madson, who is a former professor emerita at Stanford University, recommends just trying to be average, which releases the volcano of built-up pressure most teachers feel every day they pull into the parking lot. It allows you to breathe and removes the stress of feeling as if you have to be perfect. It wards off the judgmental, worrying, and self-defeating thoughts that straitjacket your personality and eclipse your joy.

Although your expectations of students will remain high, you'll take it easy on yourself. In other words, *don't* try your best. This advice may seem counterintuitive given all the high-pressure messages teachers receive about test scores, urgency, and the like, but the effect is transformational and liberating.

At first, it can be hard to wrap your head around: To be most effective, you must *not* try hard to be effective. Madson says, "Do what is natural, what is easy, what is apparent to you. Your unique view will be a revelation to someone else." She goes on to advise that if you just show up, the magic will happen. Again, this doesn't mean that you'll arrive late or fail to prepare your materials, schedules, or objectives for the day. It just means that when you open your mouth to speak, you'll do so without feeling as if you have to do something monumental to get your students' attention.

Saturday Night Live alumna Kristen Wiig says of improvisation, "It's a combination of listening and trying *not* to be funny." The same principle applies to teaching. Instead of thinking, working, rushing, and struggling, rely on what you already have inside. Trust in yourself and in your hard-earned knowledge of content. Take the pressure off and your performance and ability to inspire students will soar. You'll also be a lot happier and healthier.

The last and most important principle is to be attentive while in the midst of your teaching day. More than just being in the moment, attentiveness entails having an awareness of the entire picture. The most extraordinary teachers are also the most observant.

They are alert and cognizant of everything that is happening out-side of themselves. They brush aside their private thought life and employ their full array of senses. This allows them to adjust their teaching and react in perfect relevance to their students. It allows them to know when to pause, when to challenge, and when to back off. It gives them a feel for the energy of the room in order to control the ebb and flow and adjust accordingly. It informs their every decision and gives them maximum control over learning and behavior. It's the information that enters in through the senses that fuels their timing and stories and levels of work that match precisely what their students need.

Placing the highest priority on observation will tell you so much more about your students than reams of test-score data. It also encourages better behavior, maturity, and tenacious in-dependence. It shocks me when visiting classrooms how oblivi-ous most teachers are. They're so consumed with strategies *that make little to no difference* that they can't see what their students need from moment to moment. Many blunder on talking and shuffling papers without ever noticing that they've lost control of their class. Teacher unawareness is a direct, and often main, cause of dissatisfaction, boredom, and malaise. Once your stu-dents enter your classroom, it's best to shut down all thoughts of past and future and turn your observational powers fully on and toward them.

Roald Amundsen once said that victory awaits he who has everything in order, and this will always be true when it comes to teaching. But your preparation must match the unique conditions of the job. Knowing how to implement curriculum and teaching strategies is necessary, without a doubt, but it's only a small part of teaching. To be a happy and effective teacher, it's content knowledge that must make up the bulk of your preparation.

The good news is that other than keeping up with trends in your field, once you're an expert you're an expert. You won't have to do much if any preparation in this regard. Your daily planning will consist almost exclusively of determining a clear objective for each lesson—which we'll cover how to do in an upcoming chapter. Because once you know what you want your students to understand, or be able to do, you're going to let your natural wisdom take over.

You're going to clear your mind, wake up to the present, and improvise. What you need to do and say to motivate, capture, and inspire will come to you inexplicably, almost magically. You'll possess that awesome feeling of knowing you're reaching every student. Stories and anecdotes you haven't thought of for years will come spilling out to the delight and mesmerization of your class. You'll have dozens of metaphors, shortcuts, connections, and historical tidbits to choose from. You'll know what motivational buttons to push and just the right words to say.

Great teaching is about leaning on all the knowledge you've learned over a lifetime of schooling, reading, and living. It's about trusting yourself and being exactly who you are. It's about shoving all the clutter aside, living in the here and now, and letting your light shine.

Eyes closed, we're gonna spin through the stars
Our arms wide as the sky

-Dave Matthews Band, "You and Me"

"Dedication is often just meaningless work in disguise."

-Timothy Ferriss, author of *The 4-Hour Workweek*

Bridge

I like to listen to classical music when I write. I have a number of favorite Pandora stations that provide a continuous stream of selections from Mozart and Bach to modern-day composers like Rachel Portman and Patrick O'Hearn. The music is relaxing and helps drown out the ambient sounds of my neighborhood.

Because I put it on the moment I open my laptop, it helps me reach a quicker and deeper state of *flow*. It has a unique way of tunneling my vision and focusing my attention on the work in front of me. Occasionally, however, a piece of music will cut through the wall of concentration. It will cause me to turn my attention away from my work, if ever briefly, and to the extraordinary sound coming from the speakers. It doesn't happen often, but when it does, I take a break and enjoy it. "Opus 23" by Dustin O'Halloran does the trick. So do "Thursday" by Takenobu and "Adagio for Strings" by Samuel Barber. But there is one piece of music that stops me in my tracks no matter where I am or what I'm doing. And I know I'm not alone.

Composed by Claude Debussy in 1905, "Clair De Lune" is the third movement of a larger work called "Suite Bergamasque." It's often used as an example of the impressionist period of music, which ran roughly for 50 years in the late 19th and early 20th centuries. Impressionism was born out of the art movement of the same name. Artists like Monet, Degas, Renoir, and Manet sought to capture the moment in their art as they experienced it rather than relying on realism. They used light, color, and movement to depict their "impression" of what they were experiencing with their senses. Debussy, as well as other period composers like Maurice Ravel and Erik Satie, expressed themselves musically in much the same way.

Their music doesn't tell a story so much as it invokes a feeling. It isn't just nice to listen to, but has the ability to transport to another time, place, or state of mind. "Clair De Lune" or Satie's "Gymnopédie," to use another powerful example, take the experience of listening to music one step further. They bridge the gap from your head to your heart and all the way down to your tingling fingertips. The gorgeous arrangements of these two pieces of music demand the listener to stop and think and feel. They can invoke sadness or joy or contemplation, depending on your mood. They can stir memories, inspire dreams, or ignite a call to step out of your comfort zone. One thing is for sure: They can't be ignored.

The connection this beautiful music is able to make with the listener is similar to what great teachers are able to do with their lessons. They're able to not just give information, but to reach down, grab students by the lapels, and pull them into new and exciting worlds. They're able to bridge the gap so many teachers struggle to close between the staid curriculum and the attention of their class. They're able to repeat again and again those rare moments when students sit slack-jawed and silent as you read aloud a great work of literature or demonstrate a cool experiment. Their classrooms are factories of inspiration, churning out lesson after lesson that cause students to love school and *want* to listen, learn, and behave.

The reason so few teachers have this ability is because the curriculum often gets in the way. On its own, it's dry, spiritless, and uninspiring. Some of the strategies teachers are taught in professional development trainings and conferences are good, as are those found in many resources, but they lack that "Clair De Lune" ability to captivate. They lack the connection that makes the content matter to students. When teachers sit down to plan, this is the piece that is missing. This is the piece they struggle to find and insert into their lessons. Simply following the paint-by-numbers teacher's guide will leave students yawning and staring out the window.

The other problem is that the sheer volume of information teachers are given makes it difficult to pick out what is most important and interesting to students. A friend of mine who is a third grade teacher recently complained to me about a new writing program her district is adopting. The summary alone is 89 pages. The result is that teachers are spending way too much time preparing, and then when they do stand before their students, they're unable to reliably capture their attention. They don't have anything to offer that their students can latch on to and really care about.

In the prior chapters, we talked about the importance of being an expert in your subject area, and how context is key to driving students deep into your lessons. We also talked about how improvisation can make you more interesting and magnetic. This chapter is about simplifying the planning process while providing you a pathway to extraordinary teaching. It's about showing you exactly what to do with all that curricular information you've been given and how to present it in a meaningful way to your students. It's about using your expertise and natural improvisational skills to provide rich and captivating context. But first we're going to talk about time.

Cyril Northcote Parkinson was a former teacher and captain in the Queen's Royal Regiment of the British Army. He was also a prize-winning author of dozens of books about naval history and a visiting professor at Harvard, UC Berkeley, the University of Liverpool, and other colleges and universities. But he is most famous for a book that has nothing to do with the British fleet. In 1957, Parkinson wrote a book called *Parkinson's Law*, which became a bestseller.

Parkinson's Law is the tendency for organizations and individuals to expand a task in complexity and importance in relation to the time given for its completion. In other words, if you give yourself an hour to prepare for a day's teaching, then you'll fill the whole hour, often with obstacles and difficulties you would have never encountered had you allowed yourself only half the time.

This is why when you give a group of teachers half a day to come up with a school's mission statement, they'll make full use of the time. They'll tweak it and redo it and second guess themselves all the way up to the moment it must be turned in. When, in reality, they could get it done as well or better in less than 30 minutes—or even less than 10.

The law also says that when you limit the time needed to complete a task, your focus increases. You zero in on what you need to do to produce quality work. Distractions and digressions rarely enter the picture. As a result, you get it done quicker and often better than if you were to allow yourself more time.

I've experimented with this concept a lot over the years, both as a teacher and as a writer. My first two books took me a year each to complete, which was precisely the amount of time I gave myself. My most recent book, *Classroom Management for Art, Music, and PE Teachers*, however, took just five weeks, which, again, was the amount of time I allotted for its completion.

Within each day of those five weeks, I limited myself to only 90 minutes of writing. I set a timer and stuck to it. The result on my focus and productivity was eye opening. At the time, the work I seemed way too fast, and I felt as if I were writing just to fill the page. But when it came time to edit, which I also strictly limited, I had far less work to do. I didn't change much of anything. The quality of my writing improved by limiting the time I devoted to it.

The problem with applying Parkinson's Law to teaching is that it's hard to know exactly *how* to plan. Most teachers are unsure of how best to approach the task in a way that prepares them to deliver inspiring lessons. They sit down at their desk with their guides and materials without having a definitive strategy. They end up spending their time on things that ultimately don't make much difference and still feeling like they have more to do. Although setting a timer to limit planning time is still beneficial, and likely to produce better results, having a reliable approach is the key to planning great lessons in the least amount of time.

Danielle was a teacher from the American South who signed up for two consecutive hours of personal coaching with me in early 2016. When we met via Skype, Danielle spent the first twenty minutes describing her class. She talked about how her students weren't necessarily poorly behaved. Her classroom wasn't chaotic, and her students seemed to like her well enough. But there was a buzz of tension that never seemed to leave the room. Her students didn't listen well. They were distracted and talkative. Motivation was low and they appeared bored with the curriculum and bored with her when she presented her lessons. They were preoccupied with everything but their schoolwork.

Moreover, Danielle was stressed out and spending way too many hours at school. She conceded that although she tried to make her lessons interesting, she knew this was an area of weakness. She just didn't know where to begin. After making minor adjustments to her classroom management plan and reviewing the most effective way to enforce consequences, we set about making her lessons more compelling for her students. We gave her a plan of attack that would cut her preparation time in half, while at the same time ensuring her curriculum resonated with students.

After just two weeks, Danielle reported that her teaching life had changed. Her students were no longer distracted and itching to talk during lessons. They were no longer bored and daydreaming. Instead, they were engaged. They were motivated to learn. They were eager to participate and behaved much calmer throughout the day.

When it was time to shift responsibility to them and their work (which we'll cover in chapter 8), they got down to it quickly and with more focus than she had ever seen before. The best part is that she was having a lot more fun. She was more open and free to be herself and let her personality shine. She was improvising, playacting, and telling stories her students couldn't get enough of. She was the inspiring teacher she always wanted to be. She was also going home a lot earlier and with more energy.

The approach to planning and connecting with students I explained to Danielle is the same approach I've used myself for more than 20 years. It works whether you're an elementary, middle, or high school teacher. It works regardless of your subject area or what neighborhood you teach in. It works no matter what materials you've been given to prepare your lessons.

It consists of only three steps that simply and reliably bridge the gap between your lifeless curriculum and your students. It doesn't, however, affect the methods you wish to use when allowing your students to practice what you've taught them. When you shift responsibility, you can still choose a variety of ways they can prove they understand your objective. You can still have them work in groups preparing projects and presentations or you can have them working independently or in pairs. The focus of the three steps is on your presentation to your class. It's on the moment you step in front of your students to deliver your lesson. It's the moment teachers struggle with the most.

As long as I've been a teacher, the thrust of educational reform has been about teachers doing more. It's been about adding more and giving more. It's been about increase, expansion, and complexity. It's been about filling the day with more and more strategies. But to be an effective teacher, you must do the opposite.

In his book, *The ONE Thing*, Gary Keller makes the argument that the secret to success in any field is to go small and simple. It's to focus on what is most important and has the greatest effect, and then doing it really, really well (i.e. the 80/20 rule). The result is not only better performance, but also more time and less stress. The three-step process to planning and carrying out inspiring lessons is based on this principle. The idea is to narrow in on what you want your students to know or be able to do, and then deliver the information they need to be successful in a compelling way. It's to cut out the 80 percent of fat and fluff and do only what matters.

The first step is to select a single, solitary objective. You've no doubt heard this many times before, but so many teachers forget the importance of choosing *just one thing* for their students to understand or accomplish per lesson. It's okay for your students to use the skills they've learned from previous lessons, which are smart to review, but anything new should boil down to one goal.

Sadly, with many of the guides and resources available to teachers, the objective isn't always easy to spot, or even given at all, in which case you must select one yourself. This is critical because it will drive every word that comes out of your mouth and every action you take. I don't care how good of a speaker you are, if you don't have a clear objective, your students will be confused. Your improvisational tangents will be all over the place.

So, for every lesson you teach, the first thing you must do when you sit down to plan is identify a single objective. When you write it down in your lesson plan book, be sure to use simple and clear language. The more distinct and understandable the objective is in your mind, the more effective you'll be in presenting it to your students.

The second step is to find *one thing* noteworthy about your objective or topic that you can "sell" to your students. You're going to look for what is cool, interesting, disgusting, fascinating, weird, beneficial, sad, funny, scary, amazing, or otherwise worth learning about. There is *always* something. No matter how boring you believe your objective to be, there is always something related that you can find that will get your students to sit up and take notice.

Now, when you first step in front of your class to deliver your lesson, it's a good idea not to reveal too much about your one thing of note. You always want to leave a bit of mystery. *"I'm going to show you something today you're not going to believe!" "You're going to hear a story that will make your skin crawl." "We're going to learn a skill that will instantly make you a better reader."*

The wonderful thing about having a noteworthy aspect to each lesson is that it will excite you, too. It will automatically tap into that part of you that loves to teach. It will give you the opportunity to bring passion to your lessons. It will also keep you focused on your objective and naturally lead to the next step. It will conjure images, feelings, and memories that you're then going to use to bring depth and substance to your lesson in a way that will mesmerize your students.

The third and final step is to add connections from your teaching materials, life experiences, and expert knowledge of your subject that fulfill the noteworthy part of your lesson. *This* is teaching. It's the difference between your students clamoring to learn, and staring off into the distance. It's the context, meaning, relevance, and excitement that makes what you have to teach your students matter to them. It's Jessica Mendoza providing the viewer fascinating history and insider information. It's painting a word picture so the commuters at the L'Enfant train station appreciate the genius of Joshua Bell. It's researching the little-known backstory of the Gettysburg Address or the near failure of the Hubble telescope. It's what you'll spend most of your teaching thought life on.

Although details and descriptions add great interest to your lessons, and by themselves are remarkably effective, it's storytelling that puts students over the edge.

Scientists have long understood that the Broca and Wernicke areas of the brain are where we interpret language. They are where we turn words into meaning. But recently, researchers have discovered that stories not only activate the Broca and Wernicke regions, but also the areas of the brain that deal with smell, touch, motion, and body movement.

It turns out that when we listen to stories, our brain reacts as if we are right there in the world or scene being described, experiencing it as if we're an actual participant. We create visualizations of what we are hearing. We feel the mood, the tone, and the emotion of the moment. Sights, smells, and moving pictures become part of the experience. It's not only meaning that we interpret, but also impression. It's the chill on a snowy mountaintop. The exotic sounds of the Amazon rainforest. The sweaty-palmed tension of an awkward meeting between two former best friends.

Stories stimulate connections in the listener and have been shown to improve empathy and social skills, deepen understanding, and prompt predictions all the way up to a resolution.

Nothing I've ever done as a teacher has had greater impact on learning, behavior, and enjoyment of school than storytelling. It's not even close. But if you're new to storytelling, it can be intimidating. So many teachers think that you need to have a special talent or extensive training as a stage actor to pull it off consistently. It can also be difficult to know where and how to come up with stories. It isn't unusual to think that it may take *more* planning time, not less, to come up with a story.

First, know that anything told in story form will be more powerful than providing the information outright. So never get hung up on worrying how good your stories are. Not every story has to be *The Chronicles of Narnia* and not every story has to have the five elements of character, setting, plot, conflict, and resolution. They can be simple observations and anecdotes that add more context to your objective. They can be a short spiel about Pythagora's theorem, an imaginary yarn about a girl visiting the ruins of Pompeii, or a memory from your childhood.

Sometimes the story you tell will be right out of the teacher's guide. Now, it may not always look like a story, but it doesn't take much to take the information and tell it as a story. *"When I opened the teacher's guide the other day, this lesson reminded me of the time I first learned how to divide fractions . . ."* Your story doesn't even have to have a direct link. In fact, the more unlikely and unusual the connection is to your objective, the more compelling the story will be. This surprising fact is also the secret to finding great stories.

I began this chapter with a story about classical music because it interests me, but I could have begun the chapter in dozens of different ways. I could have related a story about archery and the connection between the shooter and the feel of the arrow feathers along the jawline. I could have told a story about my wife's spaghetti and its connection to her Italian heritage. The topic of the story may have nothing to do with the topic of the lesson, but if there is an analogy, then you have a story that will engross and enlighten your students, as well as deepen their understanding.

The truth is, you can choose just about any topic in the world and find an analogy to fit your objective. Your stories don't even have to be true. I've found that stories with a supernatural element tend to be especially powerful. I've told multi-part stories about leprechauns, superheroes, and snakes that talk. Shoot for something out of left field, and you'll have your students on the edge of their seat.

Storytelling is much easier than most people realize. You can't really mess it up. A good way to start is with short narratives that introduce your lesson or topic. It's a great way to capture initial interest. Once you have your students' attention, then you can transition to the heart of your lesson.

As for planning your story, sketch out on paper only the main elements of what you want to say. I usually write a single word or short phrase at most to represent the story I'm going to tell. It's important that you let your improvisational skills do the rest. In fact, if you plan a story too much, it will inhibit your natural charisma. Know the arc of your story, but not the precise words or actions you'll use to tell it. I know this sounds haphazard, but once you get the hang of it, it will transform your teaching and make planning reliably interesting lessons a snap. Trust yourself and your natural ability to improvise, and your personality and passion will shine through. Your likability, drama skills, and humor will go through the roof, and you'll have far greater influence on your students.

The three steps provide a definitive plan for transforming your lifeless curriculum into lessons your students will love taking part in. They bridge the gap. They connect the disconnect. They free you to apply Parkinson's Law and get your planning done in half the time. But most importantly, they'll enable you to do your part in the learning process exceedingly well, so that when you shift responsibility to your students to apply what they've learned, they'll eagerly take it.

"Vision without action is a daydream.
Action without vision is a nightmare."

-Japanese proverb

"The most pathetic person in the world is
someone who has sight, but has no vision."

-Helen Keller

Envision

Twenty minutes before the start of a race, Lindsey Vonn, the winningest skier in World Cup history, finds a quiet spot behind the starting gate. She dons her helmet and goggles, snaps into her skis, and loops the ski pole straps around her wrists. She takes a few deep breaths and then does something onlookers find bizarre. She closes her eyes, bends into a semi-crouch, and begins slowly weaving her head to and fro. She reaches one hand out in front of her and it too begins to wheel, dip, and turn, as her body sways along with the motion.

She'll continue in this manner for a minute or so, or about the time it will take her to ski down the mountain. A moment later her eyes will open. She'll straighten, make a quick check of the time, and then do it all over again. She'll run through the same oddball movements 10 or 15 times before stepping into the starting gate. At first glance, it looks like she's grooving along to music, perhaps trying to relax and focus before the race. But what she is doing is far more purposeful and one of the keys to her success. She is visualizing herself negotiating every turn, rise, and jump from start to finish. She is seeing herself in her mind's eye, following a predetermined line down the mountain that will give her the best chance of winning.

Long before the actual race, Vonn and her coaches will study the course. They'll pore over maps, test snow conditions, and inspect every section along the way. She'll then take practice runs to get a feel for the optimal path to take around and over the obstacles. She'll make equipment choices, consult her coaches and trainers, and come up with a plan of attack. In the evenings, and while relaxing between practice sessions, Vonn will do hundreds of visualization exercises. She and her team do all this pre-race work so that when she bursts from the gate at the top of the mountain, she can rely exclusively on her ability, instinct, and muscle memory.

Because she knows every inch of the course, she can relax, clear her mind, and focus on finishing the run in the fastest possible time. It gives her the confidence to race at full speed without worrying about something coming up she is unprepared for.

Athletes in a wide range of sports use visualization because research has shown that it can train cognitive processes like attention, perception, motor control, and memory nearly as well as actual practice, but without the stress on the body. It can also increase motivation and help the performer get into a faster and deeper state of *flow*—which has been shown to vastly improve performance. But visualization isn't just for athletes. Salespeople, artists, actors, marketers, clothing designers, police officers, and scores of other professions also benefit from visualization. And so can teachers, and in a big way.

It does, however, have limitations. Self-help gurus and motivational speakers from as far back as the 1930s have recommended a particular form of visualization whereby the practitioner pictures an outcome or goal already having been reached. So, for example, instead of visualizing the skiing portion of her event, Lindsey Vonn would picture the glorious moments afterward. She would imagine the feelings of success. She would see herself receiving the gold medal and basking in the glow of her victory.

You've no doubt heard of this type of visualization. A few years ago it got a rash of publicity following the publication of a book called *The Secret*. Visualizing success is still popular today and extolled in countless books, talk shows, and magazine articles. Enthusiasts tout the power of picturing yourself in a big house, driving a fancy car, or lying on the beach in Bora Bora. Indulging in these fantasies, the idea goes, will make them more likely to come true.

Science, however, is now proving what you probably already knew: It's a bunch of hooey. In fact, visualizing success can make you *less* likely to accomplish your goals. The warm feelings it invokes remove the motivation to pursue what you want to accomplish. It also leaves you unprepared to tackle the realities and obstacles along the way, leads to disappointment and discouragement, and underscores the shallowness of focusing on the fruits of success rather than the intrinsic value of the journey.

In 1958, a former teacher named Gene Bauer began planting daffodils in the hills surrounding her home in the San Bernardino Mountains. She continued to plant year after year for the next 50 years—some hundreds of thousands of bulbs. Before retiring in 2009, Gene and her husband would open her beautiful garden to visitors from the last week of March to mid-April. The garden was the subject of numerous newspaper and magazine stories over the years, and at least two books. It even made the rounds as a viral email in the late 1990s.

The story of one woman planting one flower at a time to create this magnificent 5-acre landscape resonated with people around the world. It was a lesson in the importance of focusing on the process rather than the destination. It also showed people in a striking way that with small steps you can leverage big results. When Gene planted her first bulb, she didn't have in mind the finished product. Doing so would have been overwhelming. Instead, she focused her attention on the joy of the actual work. She reveled in the fresh mountain air and being around the beauty she created.

It is this focus on process that is the secret to effective visualization. Now, it's important to note that visualization isn't a spiritual discipline. It isn't meditation or mysticism or parapsychology. It's nothing more than a tool for better performance—whether on the ski slope, during a sales call, or in the classroom. It's also easy and natural. You're already doing it to some degree.

Dana Sinclair, a performance psychologist who works with actors, athletes, musicians, and lawyers describes visualization as something people do all the time. When we think about doing anything in the future, feelings and images naturally pop into our head. We visualize before going to the grocery store or picking a friend up from the airport or heading out for a walk in the neighborhood.

When we make it purposeful, however, like Lindsey Vonn, we're then able to do these things smoother and far more efficiently. That isn't to say that you have to review your lesson plans hundreds of times in your head or think through every moment of the school day. Just a little visualization is all you need to reap the many benefits.

Dr. Teodor Grantcharov is a laparoscopic surgeon from Toronto, Canada who has been using visualization to improve his performance in the operating room since he was a resident. He spends just 5 or 10 minutes every morning mentally rehearsing the steps he'll take for each operation that day. The practice lowers his stress and makes him a better, more prepared surgeon when he walks into surgery. His success using visualization, as well as evidence from other fields, led him to organize a team of researchers to study how it can benefit future surgeons and their patients.

Grantcharov and lead author Marisa Louridas selected 20 laparoscopy residents and randomly placed them into two groups. One group received conventional training and the other group received training that included mental practice. The residents were then tested on their ability to perform a particularly challenging operation that entailed guiding a scoped instrument into the small intestine of a pig while watching images on a screen. It's an operation that Grantcharov describes as the hardest skill to teach and the most difficult to master.

The results, which were published in the *British Journal of Surgery*, were striking. In comparing the two groups, Louridas and Grantcharov found that the group that received visualization training performed considerably better, particularly when the researchers threw in a surprise emergency that required the residents to adjust on the fly. The visualization group did better because the experience felt familiar to them. Before walking into the operating room, they had already done the operation many times before in their head, which gave them a profound advantage over the other residents.

Teachers who include just a few minutes of mental practice per day, in just three areas of teaching, will also experience striking improvement. If you think back to the second chapter and the importance of saying no, one of the things you're going to say yes to is uninterrupted time alone at your desk or work area before school begins each morning. Much of this time will be devoted to lesson planning or organizing your classroom, but you can also set aside a few minutes to visualize the lessons you've already planned. This is the first area of teaching you'll want to incorporate mental practice.

Now, it's important to note that not everyone visualizes in perfect moving pictures. Sometimes you'll have flashes of images. Sometimes feelings and impressions. Sometimes the scene will jump-cut quickly from one thing to the next. Sometimes you'll be in fast motion, like a Charlie Chaplin film. Just accept whatever comes and run through your lessons from start to finish. You don't necessarily need to experience all of it. In fact, it's best that you don't. Remember, it's important that you leave room for improvisation. You just need to visualize the steps and connections along the way. Your brain will know the difference.

For example, if you have a story in mind, you may only visualize the critical elements. You may only visualize the opening, the middle arc, the conflict, and the conclusion. You may hear yourself narrating, "Okay, I'm going to do this, and then this . . . then they're going to ask questions . . . then I'm going to tell the story . . . run through the jungle . . . chased by a tiger . . . into a clearing caused by logging."

Even Lindsey Vonn skips mentally rehearsing the long and smooth sections of a racecourse. The famous photographer Ansel Adams used to visualize just the elements of the picture he wanted to create. He'd see the position of his camera, the time of day, the weather, the lighting, and the exposure he needed to reproduce the end product he had in mind.

In time, you'll be able to visualize entire lessons in less than a minute by focusing on just the important details. Like anything, visualization is a skill you'll get better at the more you practice. You'll get better as you experience how powerful and effective it is. You'll get better as you experience how accurately your actual lessons reflect your visualization of them.

Some performance experts recommend inserting sounds and smells into your visualizations, like the bustle of students entering the classroom or your morning coffee as you bring it to your lips. The idea is that the more realistic you can make the experience, the more effective it will be. I haven't personally found this to be the case. If the sights and sounds come naturally, then great, allow them in. But trying too hard can pull your focus away from process, performance, and the details of your job.

While a graduate student many years ago, I interned for the college softball team. The coach used visualization with her players before every game, but it was centered exclusively on the environment—the colors, the crowd, the weather. And while this may have made the players more comfortable stepping onto the field, it did nothing to improve their performance. A visualization of seeing a good pitch and making a smooth swing would have been a lot more effective. Focus on what you need to *do* and you'll see and experience a real difference when you step in front of your students.

The second area of teaching you'll want to visualize is your response to misbehavior. When you see yourself calmly following through and holding students accountable, then that's exactly what you'll do when it actually happens.

What is especially helpful about visualizing behavior management is that you can work on your weaknesses. You can picture that one student who so often gets on your nerves behaving in a way that normally would drive you crazy. But in your visualizations, you can practice handling it perfectly. You can picture the student being disrespectful, trying to argue with you, or denying their involvement in a recent incident and you responding effectively. You can also visualize your entire class entering your classroom excitable and unfocused, and you calmly sending them back outside to do it again properly. You can correct all of your previous missteps and mistakes and groove the best possible future reactions to them. You can create the personal habits and dispositions that are necessary to improve behavior and rid yourself of those that do the opposite.

What is particularly exciting about visualizing your reactions to disrespect, temper tantrums, arguing, interrupting, side-talking, or any other behavior is that you'll find yourself—without conscious thought—responding in the exact way you visualized. Not only will your words, voice, and body language follow the script, but you'll no longer react emotionally.

The fact is, whatever you visualize tends to come true—not because of any magic process, but because you've practiced beforehand. You've rehearsed the habits of great teaching and effective classroom management in a safe, judgment-free environment and in a way that is nearly as effective as if you were to practice it for real. Once your visualizations become just the way you do things, you'll no longer have to practice them mentally. You'll no longer have to try and tamp down your emotions or resist the stress rising up inside of you. Handling misbehavior exactly as you wish will become as natural as a stroll in your neighborhood.

The third area of teaching worth seeing in your mind's eye is the sequence and tone of your day from start to finish. This is a visualization that you'll do just before the morning bell rings. While sitting at your desk, or even standing just inside your closed door, shut your eyes and see your class entering and following your directions. See them listening intently as you go through the first lesson of the day. See every activity, transition, and movement in and out of your classroom transpire until the day ends and you send your students happily on their way.

Maintain a picture of you and the disposition you most want to see and experience. See yourself calmly enforcing consequences and passionately telling stories. See yourself teaching clear and compelling lessons, having fun, and sharing an occasional laugh with your students. See yourself observing closely as your students become immersed in their work.

This final visualization will, of course, be at an accelerated speed, and cover only the major highlights. Don't try too hard or worry about doing it perfectly. Just stay relaxed and the images will come to you without effort. Although you will get better the more you do it, you should experience immediate results. You should experience the best and smoothest day you've had in a long while.

The best news is that it's repeatable. Every day you visualize will be more efficient, effective, and enjoyable than any day you don't. One important reason for this that we haven't yet mentioned is that visualizing something beforehand frees you to live in the moment. It frees you to relax and focus on what is right in front of you.

This is an incredibly enjoyable and effective place to be, especially for teachers who are accustomed to being preoccupied with thinking one or more steps ahead. Research into this present state—also called mindfulness—has shown it to be a wonderful stress reliever and mood booster. It is also where we discover a ready-made state of *flow*, where our improvisations, humor, and charisma come pouring out.

When you visualize your lessons, your responses to misbehavior, and your school day, mindfulness will come naturally. Your day will slow down. You'll find yourself savoring the joy of teaching and making better connections with your students. Your improvisational skills will skyrocket. Your observational powers and understanding of your students and their strengths and weaknesses will also improve. You'll go about your day with the comforting feeling that, in many ways, the future is already taken care of. You already know what you're going to do from one lesson, activity, and transition to the next so clearly that you no longer have to give it much thought.

Jack Nicklaus, long considered the greatest golfer in history, once remarked that he never hit a shot, not even in practice, without having a picture of it in his head. He eliminated all mental clutter and worry over the past and future so he could let his natural ability take over. When he stepped up to the ball, he was free to let it rip. He was free to focus on process.

Watts Towers sit on a triangle of land between East 107th Street and Santa Ana Boulevard in Los Angeles as a monument to persistence. Constructed of steel and mortar and decorated with a mosaic of discarded glass, tile, sea shells, and pottery, they are the product of a visionary named Simon Rodia. Rodia was an Italian immigrant who began the project in his backyard during his off hours in 1921.

Every day for the next 33 years his solitary figure could be seen far up in the trusses, hammering and shaping his art. The site, which is now a historical landmark and cultural arts center, consists of 17 sculptures in all. Just feet from a neat row of houses, they have a stark, urban beauty and are a particularly arresting example of 20th century folk art. That one person created this wonderment without help or the benefit of machinery or scaffolding is hard to imagine. It is the largest feat of construction ever built by a single person.

As I strolled the grounds, I was moved by the care and intricate detail devoted to each small segment of the work. It was clear that Rodia was motivated by far more than the finished product. In fact, not long after completing construction, he moved away, never to set foot on the site again. It was the work that he loved. It was the purpose it gave his existence. It was the absorption in a pursuit that meant something to him and to the thousands of people like me who visit the towers every year.

Rodia created an enduring work of art by seeing in his mind's eye the position of every broken shell, glass shard, and bend of rebar, and then molding them into reality. It was his focus on the beauty and soul of process that raised the towers to their soaring height.

Like great art, great teaching isn't about just getting through the day. It's about being fully present and engaged in what's right in front of you. It's about planting daffodils, building towers, and skiing the downhill run. It's about process, persistence, and the moment-to-moment experience of being a teacher.

Visualizing just a few minutes a day will put you there. It will slow you down, fill you with confidence, and allow your talent to shine. It will put you into a quicker and deeper state of *flow*, where time slows and you inhabit your best and most effective self. The second you open your eyes after visualizing your day, you can forget about the future. You can forget about the past. You're free to inspire your students, to laugh and love, and to enjoy the journey.

"To strive, to seek, to find, and not to yield."

-Alfred Lord Tennyson, *Ulysses*

Shift

When Columbus sailed the ocean blue, he did so by following a straight line of latitude. He didn't have much of a choice. At the time, and for the next 300 years, seafaring navigators had no reliable way of determining longitude. They either stayed close to "the parallel" or risked becoming lost at sea. Still, without any longitudinal bearing, they often never knew when they reached their destination until they crashed there. They were also easy prey for pirates trolling well-known shipping lanes. Navigation became so perilous, and was so important for future trade and exploration, that in 1714 the British Parliament established a reward of several million dollars for anyone who could solve this enormous riddle of the time. Great minds like Galileo and Newton believed the answer was to be found in the heavens, among the fixed stars and revolving planetary bodies. But John Harrison thought otherwise.

Harrison was a self-educated carpenter and clockmaker from the English county of Yorkshire. It was already well established that simply knowing the time on board a moving ship, which can be determined by the sun at its highest point, and knowing the time at the home port would provide exact longitude. The difference in the two times correlated with a known separation in degrees of longitude.

The problem at the time, however, was that no clock had been invented that could withstand the harsh conditions at sea. The pitching and yawning deck would throw a pendulum clock out of whack within sight of land, and the wet, salty air would quickly deteriorate its internal mechanisms. But Harrison was undeterred. After just *thinking* about the problem for four years, he set about trying to create a clock that could keep accurate time despite the conditions. He did almost nothing else for the next 40 years. Through countless trials, setbacks, and failures, Harrison succeeded in building a clock that could reliably guide ship captains safely around the globe in any direction. In all, he built just five models, the third of which (H3) took him 19 years.

While on vacation several years ago, my wife and I took a train ride across the Thames to London's National Maritime Museum in Greenwich to see four of the timekeepers on display. They are beautiful and elegant pieces of machinery and a testament to Harrison's ingenuity. H1, H2, and H3 are still running, housed in their own plexiglass cases. H4, which requires lubrication due to its smaller size and enclosed mechanisms, sits frozen in time. As I circled these amazing works of both art and science, I was struck by the amount of dedication and perseverance it took to conceive and then build them. The single-mindedness with which Harrison approached the monumental task is an attribute common to the most successful people, regardless of the endeavor.

The willingness to put your head down and work, especially when success isn't assured, is what separates those who soldier through and overcome difficult challenges and those who don't. Far more than talent or intelligence, it is hard work that is the secret to success. It is mental toughness and dogged determination. It is a trait that psychologist Angela Duckworth and her team at the University of Pennsylvania call *grit*.

According to Duckworth, grit is the tendency to sustain interest in and effort toward longterm goals. It entails working with great persistence for years, even decades, in pursuit of a single objective. Grit has been shown to be a predictor of high school graduation rates, National Spelling Bee performance, and surviving the first difficult summer at West Point. It's also a trait lacking in many of our students, perhaps more so today than at any other time in history.

The self-esteem movement began in the late 1960s and has only gathered steam until present. Through the work of Jean Twenge at San Diego State University and Carol Dweck at the University of Stanford, parents and teachers are just now beginning to question the wisdom of false and excessive praise and its negative effects on children. Praising students for minimal effort and achievement sends the message that less than their best is not only good enough, but worthy of special recognition. It also lowers the bar of what is considered hard work. It encourages less effort, not more. It has also been shown to discourage students from challenging themselves and trying new things. It heightens the fear of failure, of losing the label they've been given since birth of being special, smart, and talented.

The result is that they quit when the going gets tough. And quitting is a terrible habit for children to get into, as each time it becomes easier and easier to throw in the towel. It also leads to what is known as a fixed mindset, which is the idea that intelligence and talent are fixed and can't be improved over time. This is a particularly damaging narrative that many of our students believe wholeheartedly. If they think that they can't improve, that their level of intelligence or talent precludes them from understanding advanced math or tackling French or making the basketball team, for example, then what motivation do they have to even try? Dweck has discovered that having a growth mindset, which is the belief that one can continue to learn and grow and achieve through hard work, is highly motivational and improves both grades in school and productivity in the workplace. Unsurprisingly, people with grit tend to also have a growth mindset rather than one that is fixed.

But false and excessive praise isn't the only culprit. The proliferation of social media and rapid-fire communication has shortened attention spans and made it more difficult for students to stay on task and motivated to pursue longterm goals. In a 2012 Pew Research survey, 87 percent of teachers polled said that new technologies are creating an easily distracted generation with short attention spans. The pull of the smartphone and its instant gratification has in many ways replaced the deep satisfaction of hard-won, incremental improvement over time. Schools trying to compete by adding more and more technology and encouraging more of its use hasn't helped. In the same study, 64 percent of teachers said that the latest technologies do more to distract students than help them academically.

The growing pressure on teachers to do more and be more for their students has also had a negative effect on grit and work habits. It seems every month there is a new approach or new way to teach which entails adding something rather than taking something away. Teaching gets more complex, more detailed, and more stressful every day. There is a great emphasis on "meeting the needs" of individual students rather than providing great instruction. The unintended effect is that teachers have taken on more and more responsibility for student behavior, performance, and work habits while students are taking on less and less.

This has pulled teachers away from the front of the room and direct instruction, and brought them kneeling down beside one individual student after another. It's common for teachers to be more burdened with a student's progress than the student themself. In many classrooms, teachers carry the weight of a grand piano on their shoulders while students gad about without a care in the world. We've become so focused on setting students up for success that we've forgotten what it takes to succeed. We've forgotten that it's hard work *by the student* that leads to success. In the process, we've burned out scores of teachers and done a disservice to our students.

When I was in high school I had an English teacher named Bill Heyde. In his class, you worked. Period. You were either reading, writing, or diagramming sentences for extended periods of time. His lessons to start each class, however, were dynamic. He was a remarkable speaker and communicator. He was funny and told stories and provided vivid context to the books we read. The discussions that followed were smart and natural and driven by the preparation expected of the students. He would do his part by teaching these fascinating lessons, but then turn his students loose to do their own work.

I can remember bringing essays to him over and over again. He'd mark them up and rewrite sections in just a minute or two and then send me back to grind away some more. I spent hours and hours at his kitchen table on the weekends with a few other students while he cooked, watched baseball, or worked around the house. Occasionally he'd pop in, scribble up my essay with suggestions and corrections, and then move on to something else.

It wasn't unusual to spend weeks on a single assignment through a dozen rewrites. This approach was incredibly effective and Bill is a legend at my former high school and throughout the state of Missouri, where I grew up. As was mentioned in a previous chapter, it was his deep understanding of the material, and skill in delivering it, that motivated students to put in so much hard work. I last sat in his classroom a very long time ago, but I remember it so vividly because it had a profound effect on my life, my teaching, and my view of education. Those four years learning from him provided me a template for extraordinary teaching. Bill Heyde's approach did principally two things that had such an effect on his students and their future endeavors. First, he slowly built up their perseverance muscles. He built up their stamina for concentrated work and for working through difficult conundrums over time. He turned more and more of the class time over to students to allow them to practice the craft he was so magnetically teaching them.

In his 2010 book, *Talent is Overrated*, Geoff Colvin relates the story of psychologist Anders Ericsson and his quest to discover why some violinists are better than others. He visited The Music Academy of West Berlin, which had compiled reams of fascinating data about its students. After poring over the information, Ericsson was able to divide the violinists into three groups: Outstanding students who would become renowned soloists like Joshua Bell, good students who would one day work professionally as part of an orchestra, and average students who would become teachers rather than performers.

Taking into account all other variables, the results were clear and surprising. Talent had nothing to do with it. The best students had practiced an average of 10,000 hours, the next best group had practiced 8,000 hours, and the bottom group a mere 4,000 hours. Most remarkably, there were no outliers. No student in the top group practiced less than 10,000 hours and no student who practiced 10,000 hours was out of the top group. Bill Heyde intuitively knew, long before Ericsson's research, that time spent actually writing, in deliberate practice, made us better writers. The same is true of every educational endeavor or subject matter.

The second thing Bill Heyde did was build deep confidence in our ability to improve—and not just in writing. When you see the proof of your continuing progression, which Bill was quick to provide, you inevitably conclude that your ability to learn virtually anything, and attain a high level of skill, is limitless. This understanding is a powerful motivator. Just knowing that setbacks, obstacles, frustrations, and even failures are normal, even necessary, empowers you to plow through to the next level. One of the secrets to success is just knowing that you can, which will never come simply because someone tells you that you can. It may give you an initial push, if it's sincere, but its effect will only get you so far. You must see the proof yourself. You must see the difference hard work and concentrated practice can make with your own eyes. You must see it as part of your daily school experience.

When I was a fourth grade teacher, I would measure the height of each student in my class during the first week of school, cutting a length of string to represent the result. The students would then take their string and pack it in a large envelope along with an art project, a writing assignment, and a math assessment. They also would include a list of their favorite things, like movies, books, food, and places to go. On the last day of school I'd pull out these time capsules, which they had forgotten about, to show them how far they'd come. The difference was always shocking. They would laugh and their eyes would bug out as they compared their work and preferences from then to now. It was great fun, but the purpose was to drive home the point that through hard work and perseverance they can make incredible strides.

But you mustn't wait an entire year to show your students how much they're improving. It's always worth giving them an opportunity to compare their newly finished project, essay, or presentation video with the one before. Doing so gets students excited, motivated, and determined to tackle the next challenge with greater effort.

In most classrooms these days, students aren't made to practice enough to build up their stamina for hard work or generate true confidence in their abilities. Because the teacher has so much invested in their success, and feels so much pressure for them to do well, they end up filling the time with their over-support. They repeat themselves again and again. They re-teach the same things over and over. They give too many clues, offer too much help, and accept far less than what is possible. They micromanage and talk their students through every this and that.

Independent work times shrink further and further while teacher-led charting, brainstorming, diagramming, discussions, and guidance increase. The teacher then buzzes around the room stressed and overwhelmed, kneeling down to help one student after another, while many students sit idle and bored, frozen by learned helplessness.

It isn't unusual for a great many students to get through entire days without doing any real, deliberate practice. Listening and attentiveness also suffer because students have learned that the teacher will always repeat, re-teach, and spoon-feed the curriculum to them. This unburdening students of responsibility also extends to behavior, with teachers cajoling, pleading, lecturing, and trying to convince students to behave instead of allowing them to feel the weight of their behavior choices.

The secret to improving grit is to shift responsibility for learning and behaving in full to your students. It's doing your part by teaching compelling lessons through meaningful stories, connections, and context, and then letting your students loose to write the essay, perform the experiment, or solve for x with only reluctant additional support from you. It's giving your students increasing amounts of time to work, ponder, wrestle with, and overcome the challenges you place before them. It's planning projects, assignments, and presentations that take multiple steps and days, if not weeks, to complete. It's giving them the tools they need to do the work, and then letting them do it.

This also changes the way students view their school work—from busywork to get through to goals to be reached. And having tangible goals is very, very healthy. It keeps them focused and content and filled with purpose. It makes them tenaciously interested in their projects, papers, and experiments. It also calms nervous energy, gives them a deep sense of satisfaction, and makes the down time a lot sweeter.

Great teaching in action often doesn't look like much. After a clear and concise (and inspired) directed lesson, the teacher is usually found off to one side, a step or two back, perhaps even leaning against the wall. They're calm, quiet, and deeply focused on observing their class. As long as the students are working, whether in groups or individually, they'll say nothing. They'll scarcely move, because they're intent on not interfering with the experience of deep learning. They're intent on not interfering with the concentration needed to work through difficulties and conundrums.

They won't shuffle papers on their desk, pace around the room, or become lost in thought. They merely observe, learn intimately about their students and their strengths and weaknesses, and consider the focus of the next day's lesson. If a student gets stuck, they may occasionally offer a small clue or suggestion to get them going. They may whisper, "You can do it. I believe in you." They may do nothing at all to see if the student can work through it on their own. Any and all praise given is based solely on effort or work that exceeds what the student or group of students has done before.

Most of the teachers I see as part of my coaching practice are at the end of their rope. They're strung out and exhausted. Some cry softly as they relate what it's like to spend a day in their shoes. Some can barely look up to meet my eyes. But over the course of our hour-long session, as I explain how and why they need to shift more, sometimes a lot more, responsibility to their students, their posture begins to change. Their eyes clear and brighten. Relief rains down upon them in a torrent.

It's best to think of teaching as a two-way street. You give your best to your students. You teach compelling lessons. You capture interest through your passion, your humor, your stories and connections. You point out the beauty, drama, triumph, and heartache. You emote and dance and playact and bring your subject to life for your students. You *teach*. And then you turn the reins over to them. You shift the responsibility for learning in total to your students. You let them grow and mature and develop the grit they need to compete at the next level and beyond. You give them the gift of a growth mindset. You send them on their way after a year with you prepared to work at and succeed in any endeavor they choose.

This is great teaching. It isn't stress or martyrdom. It isn't pleading or crossing your fingers. It isn't yelling, lecturing, or dreading your drive in to work every day. But it does take a difference in the way you view education and how you respond to what you hear in workshops and professional trainings. It takes your own form of grit to swim against the tide, to deny your every instinct to rush to a student's side when they're struggling, to refuse the internal call to constantly do more and be more for your students. The good news is that once you begin to see the radical transformation in your students, once you experience the deep fulfillment of extraordinary teaching, you'll never go back. Your sea change will be complete.

John Harrison finished his final marine timekeeper when he was 79 years old. H5 sits on a threadbare pillow of red velvet inside a simple wooden box. It's on display at the Science Museum in South Kensington, London, a short walk from Hyde Park. At just a fraction of the size of his first three chronometers, and smaller still than H4, it looks more like a pocket watch than a clock. The dial is arrayed with Roman numerals upon a soft white face and is housed in sterling silver. A small brass star wreathes the center pin from which common arrow hands point out the time.

Although tasteful and elegant, the timepiece itself isn't much to look at. It doesn't draw crowds like the *Rosetta Stone* or *Magna Carta* at the nearby British Museum, and it doesn't occupy its own exhibit room. But there it sits, as quiet and resolute as Harrison himself, representing not just one of the greatest scientific inventions of the time, but the matchless value of grit, perseverance, and a growth mindset.

I was on the inside
When they pulled the four walls down
I was looking through the window
I was lost, I am found

-U2, "I Will Follow"

Sway

After many years as an elementary school teacher, both in the classroom and as a PE specialist, I made the jump to teaching high school. It's been a wonderful experience and, although there are certainly differences between the two levels of teaching, they're far more similar than I imagined. In the end, kids are kids and people are people. We're all looking for inspiration and purpose in our lives.

Along with the change in grade level also came a change in my daily schedule. For the first time in 25 years, I'm only teaching for half a day. I write and coach teachers during the other half of the day. Typically, I arrive to school around noon. After finding a spot in the cramped parking lot, I stop in at the school office to say hello, check my mailbox, and sign in for the day. Just beyond the office, there is a small kitchen that opens to a large media and conference room. And it was in this room, shortly after signing in one day, that I had an unnerving experience.

One of the differences between elementary and high school students is that the little ones are more openly friendly. They'll yell your name at the top of their lungs from all the way across campus just to say hello, despite having seen you just 10 minutes before. High school students, on the other hand, are extremely conscious of how they appear in front of their classmates. This isn't a criticism. It's just part of growing up. I've definitely found them as friendly as younger students, but just not as overtly demonstrative about it. After all, they have to maintain their social credibility. When they're with a group of friends, they're especially cautious and will rarely even look up when you pass by. Which is why on this particular day I was startled when I noticed out of the corner of my eye a girl watching me intently.

I was passing through the kitchen area on my way out of the office and to my classroom. She was sitting with a large group of friends, several of whom were in one of my classes. She was looking at me and smiling from ear to ear like we were old friends. There was an unabashed familiarity in her expression and body language that suggested that we not only knew each other quite well, but had experienced something profound together, like surviving a cataclysmic disaster or a couple of days stuck in an elevator.

She displayed a level of trust that typically only family members and the closest friends share. But I was new to the school, and because it was a good distance from my previous assignment, I hadn't known a single student beforehand. I turned my head and met her gaze and did the only thing I could think of to do. I smiled back and said hello. She smiled broader as her friends looked on as puzzled as I was and said, "You don't remember me do you?"

I quickly rifled through my memory files searching for a match, but nothing came up. The experience was odd. Clearly, based on her behavior, she was a long-lost cousin or maybe she had mistaken me for the guy who saved her mother or father's life during the Gulf War. "I'm sorry," I said. "Where do I know you from?" Her face sank to the floor. She was crushed I hadn't remembered her. Now I was convinced she had the wrong person. I definitely would have recognized anyone who knew me well enough to be hurt by my lack of recognition. But after a long and frustrating sigh, she held both hands up and yelled, "You were my second grade PE teacher!"

Now, it's important to mention that as a specialist who saw 400-600 students per week, I've taught many thousands of students over the years. Where I taught previously, many would come back to visit and greet me with the question, "Do you remember me?" In nearly every case, there was something about their eyes that produced a quick recognition. I would see a flash of what they looked and sounded like when I last saw them. I also had the benefit of knowing for sure that I knew them. Context is the best jog for the memory. But with this particular student, who I hadn't seen in seven years, the image didn't come quite so readily. After hearing where I knew her from, though, I was able to see her as an energetic seven-year-old running around on the playground.

What was so strange about the experience was that I hardly knew her then. When you teach so many classes a week, there are many students that you never even have a conversation with, let alone memorize their name. Yet, even sitting among friends, this student, who I hadn't seen or spoken to since she was half her current age, looked up at me as if I were a trusted confidant.

I asked her about her grades and spoke to her with the same authority I do with my current students. She shared with me that she had been struggling, and admitted that she hadn't been taking school seriously. I told her that I was going to keep tabs on her and expected her to improve her grades from here on out. It was little different than a conversation I might have had with her when she was in second grade. The influence I acquired as her once-per-week PE teacher seven years ago was as strong now as it was then. It wormholed through the years, unaffected by time. It is, in fact, a powerful and predictable force that can drive students to thought and action who have no intention of budging.

When I was a child I used to help my dad with small jobs around the house. My responsibilities entailed holding a flashlight over his work area or handing him the tools he asked for, which I could never seem to find. Sometimes he needed an extra hand to lift or carry heavy items. One cold morning he roused me out of bed to help him repair a dog kennel in the backyard. A corner of the kennel had sunk into the soft ground, stressing the supports and tilting the floor. The dogs, which my dad trained as retrievers, were forced to sleep on a slant. The plan was to lift the kennel and slide several pre-cut two-by-fours under the slumping floor. The problem was that the two of us together couldn't lift the kennel more than a couple of inches.

While I stood with my arms crossed trying to figure out what we were going to do, my dad walked into the garage and returned with a six-foot iron bar. He would use the bar in winter to break up the ice that would accumulate near doors, stairs, and walkways around the property. (I would then do the shoveling.) Next, he grabbed a solid, three-sided log from a pile nearby and set it down a foot or so from the kennel to act as a fulcrum. He laid the rod over the log while cramming the tip just under the fallen floor, creating a lever. He smiled and then let me do the honors.

With no more than a shift of body weight, I was able to lift the kennel by myself while my dad slid the wooden shims into place. I was perhaps seven or eight years old at the time, and would daydream through most jobs around the house, but this time was different. That I could create so much power with so little effort was a revelation to me. From then on I looked for solutions to problems that took the least amount of time and effort. That day in the backyard was an early clue that with the right approach, you can leverage all sorts of things—even people.

In teaching circles, you hear a lot about the importance of building personal relationships with students. But rarely will you hear about how, exactly, to do that. Left to their own devices, most teachers try to engage students in conversation. They try to spend time with them and find commonalities. They try to build rapport through one-on-one interactions. Although there is nothing wrong with these efforts, they're a weak lever. They take a great deal of time to see results and are wildly unpredictable. Trying too hard to build relationships can also make students uncomfortable being around you. It can make you appear inauthentic, or even desperate, especially if like many teachers, you attempt to build rapport by tossing out pop culture references and using language common to their age group.

So, although the goal of building personal relationships to acquire better influence is a worthy one, the way teachers go about it is often awkward and ineffective. Trying to be cool or connect with students on their level, as would a friend, will backfire every time and trying to reach students one at a time is an impossibility. The good news is that there is a way to build leverage with every student in your class without spending *any* time trying to do so. It's a way that naturally draws students into your circle of influence and makes them eager to please you, learn from you, and behave for you. It's a way that makes you a leader worth following—regardless of grade level. Kindergarten students or seniors in high school, they all respond predictably to the same approach.

There are two principles that when used together provide the influence you need to have the motivated and well-behaved class you want. It doesn't matter whether you're introverted or extroverted, short or tall, inexperienced or a veteran. They'll give you the leverage to lift the heaviest load (i.e. the most difficult class) with the least amount of effort. They'll give you the feeling of walking into your classroom and *knowing* that your students will behave, follow your instructions, and give their best effort. It's the heady feeling of knowing that they'll eagerly follow you anywhere you want to take them. It is leverage with a long iron bar, and it's the best feeling in teaching.

Recently, a friend of mine sent me a CD of a concert he attended ten years before. He found it online, and knowing how much I enjoyed the same artist, he thought of me. The concert took place during an important point in his life. He went by himself and he wanted to share the experience with me. For the next few weeks we talked and emailed back and forth, sharing our favorite songs and moments during the concert. It was fun and served as another opportunity to bond. We've been friends for 30 years, and although his gesture wasn't uncommon, I couldn't help but be touched by it.

Besides sharing similar tastes in music, we also like to exchange books. If I read something I like, I'll bring it to him the next time we get together. A couple of years before, I brought him a book called *A Higher Call* by Adam Makos, which he loved as much as I did. So it just so happened that a couple of days after receiving the CD, I heard that Adam Makos was out with a new book. I just knew I had to buy each of us a copy.

I'd like to think that this is something I would have done anyway. But the truth is, because of his recent gesture, I had a strong desire to do something nice for him. Social psychologists call this desire The Law of Reciprocity. By definition, The Law of Reciprocity is the deep-seated psychological urge to pay back any nicety done to us. It's very powerful and almost impossible to resist. This is why two friends or couples who like to go to dinner together tend to alternate paying the bill. It's the reason we send birthday or holiday cards to those who send them to us and why the friendliest restaurant servers get the highest tips. It is also the first principle in creating influence with students.

As surprising as it may seem, the way to create powerful, behavior-changing influence, leverage, and rapport with your students is to be *consistently pleasant*. The other surprise is that you never again have to go out of your way to engage individual students. In fact, as mentioned before, by doing so you risk making them uncomfortable. It more often has the effect of pushing them away and causing walls to go up, than the other way around. By simply having a nice and friendly disposition, though, your students will be naturally and irresistibly drawn to you—even, or especially, the most challenging among them. They'll want to be around you and get to know you better. They'll want to say hello to you and do nice things for you. And when students come *to you*, communication, then, and further bonding becomes effortless. The words you say will have meaning and impact and will be earnestly received.

This doesn't mean that you won't be brutally honest. It doesn't mean that you'll never tell them you're disappointed or that you expect more effort from them. It just means that you'll never again react angrily to misbehavior. Be consistently kind and they'll follow you in droves. This is why that student I hadn't seen in seven years treated me like a close family member. Although I didn't know her well at all, I had leverage and influence because of The Law of Reciprocity. In time, as you become more comfortable and consistent using the principle, you'll discover that the more you resist engaging too directly, the more powerful it is. So, not only do you not have to work hard to build relationships, it's best that you don't. There is, however, a catch.

You see, The Law of Reciprocity also works the other way. So, for example, if someone perceives you to be mean to them, they'll have the desire to be mean to you right back. This is why when someone cuts us off in traffic, it's so hard not to want to do the same to them. But here's the kicker, and the reason so many teachers struggle with classroom management: When someone has formed a negative opinion of you based on your behavior or an incident or a comment you made to them, it's hard to change their mind. It's hard to win them back over. It takes time and patience and still sometimes never happens.

Years ago, before I was married, a neighbor couple made dinner for me. It was a gorgeous paella. In their culture, particularly when there are invited guests, you take your time over dinner. You talk and share stories and linger over the meal, sometimes for a few hours. Well, I'm embarrassed to admit that I left their house too early. Even when thanking them, it felt rude. It was rude. I felt terrible about it, and from their subsequent behavior, I knew I hurt and disappointed them. I tried to engage them in conversation when I'd see them out in their front yard and invite them to my own home, but they were having none of it. I never was able to return our friendship to the level it was before the dinner.

It is the same with your students. For every time you scold them, glare at them, or even give them the cold shoulder, you set your relationship back eons, sometimes irrevocably. Remember, the principle states that you must be *consistently* pleasant, not just pleasant some of the time or even most of the time. I know this seems impossible or even unrealistic given some of the behaviors you may see in your classroom. But here's the thing: The next principle makes actually doing it, every day of the year, not only possible, but entirely doable.

The second principle is trust. Your students must trust you implicitly. They must know that when you say something, or say that you're going to do something, your words and actions are gold. This principle manifests itself most importantly in the form of your classroom management plan. By having a set of rules that cover every potential misbehavior, and by enforcing them 100 percent of the time, you're free from being in a position of creating friction or animosity with your students. In other words, you're going to let your classroom management plan do the heavy lifting for you, so you're never compelled to react in anger or frustration.

It's key, though, that you follow through calmly and dispassionately. Your students must know that it isn't personal, that there are never hard feelings, and that forgiveness is always extended.

If you add a lecture, a sarcastic remark, or your two cents worth, you'll risk reversing The Law of Reciprocity. You'll risk sabotaging your relationship and interfering with the accountability process. Being consistent and faithful to the boundaries of the class, without becoming angry or trying to coerce students to behave, engenders deep trust and respect.

Combined with your pleasant personality, it's the secret to forever ridding your classroom of misbehavior. It also encourages self-reflection, protects your students from disruption and interference, and creates a learning environment they all love being part of. So many students privately dislike their teacher because they don't safeguard their right to learn and enjoy school. This creates resentfulness and the desire to misbehave behind your back. Allow your classroom management plan to stand sentry every minute of the school day, and misbehavior will dissipate and your influence will grow.

When I first have this discussion about trust and consistency with my coaching clients, some will express doubt whether they can actually do it. They'll assume that it takes great willpower or personal discipline to override their inclination to take misbehavior personally. But I've found that simply having the knowledge of how important it is and why it works is enough to try it long enough for it to become a habit. The other force at work is that once they see how profoundly it changes their classroom, and experience how light they feel after removing such a heavy and stressful burden, they never turn back.

By allowing their classroom management plan to take care of accountability, they never again have the urge to finger-wag a student or show their personal displeasure. It effectively eliminates their own feelings of negative reciprocity. The love and respect pouring in from every corner of their classroom overcomes years, even decades, of trying to convince, admonish, and intimidate students into behaving. They discover that battling with students isn't really who they are, but was merely a crutch to try and get them through each day. Being pleasant and friendly and enjoying their students is who they are and what they always hoped to be.

The West Side Line was a mile and a half section of train track that wound through the Chelsea neighborhood of Manhattan. Disused since 1980, the track had become a crumbling remnant by the mid-1990s. As Chelsea began transforming into a popular area for art galleries and restaurants, many people living in the neighborhood, as well as former New York mayor Rudolph Giuliani, were hellbent on tearing it down. In the fall of 1999, Joshua David and Robert Hammond formed a group called Friends of the High Line in the hope that they could persuade the city to save the old tracks and turn them into a linear park similar to the one recently created on an abandoned rail line in Paris called the Promenade plantée.

Their efforts were slow going in the beginning. The biggest obstacle was convincing people what the High Line could become. Explaining it could never do their vision justice. It wasn't until a photographer named Joel Sternfeld climbed up onto the viaduct and began photographing what he saw that the proposal began gaining traction. Sternfeld's stunning images of wildflowers, sumacs, and shrubs winding amid the buildings attracted interest in the project and provided proof that it could be a benefit to the city. Today, the High Line is a beautiful park of walking paths, gardens, relaxation benches, and wide-open views of downtown. Although David, Hammond, and Friends of the High Line were the engine that propelled the project forward, it was the influence of Joel Sternfeld and his photographs that turned the tide. It was one simple thing, one force that moved people to action.

It's striking how tense and uptight so many teachers become the moment they step in front of their students. These are open and lovely people who turn unrecognizable at the sound of the morning bell. The burden of having to convince students to behave makes them wary and anxious. It buttons up their personality and pulls their attention away from inspiring students and enjoying their job.

The two principles of influence will free you to be yourself every moment of the day. They'll free you to laugh and improvise and make your relationships even stronger and more influential. Like Joel Sternfeld's images, it's the Law of Reciprocity, combined with your unwavering trustworthiness, that moves and influences students. Together, they're the arm and fulcrum that allow you to speak and teach and interact in a classroom where every student wants to please you. They're the foundation upon which you build a classroom both you and your students love coming to every day.

"We have two ears and one mouth and we should use them proportionally."

-Susan Cain, author of *Quiet: The Power of Introverts in a World That Can't Stop Talking*

Listen

The Khumbu Icefall is a heaving and crumbling sweep of glacier that sits at the base of the most popular route to the summit of Mount Everest. Although the icefall marks just the beginning of the climb, it has long been considered its most dangerous section. Climbers must use up to 60 eight-foot ladders and 6,000 feet of rope to negotiate a labyrinth of seracs, crevasses, and ice blocks as tall as office buildings. It takes between three and four hours of intense concentration to cross the expanse. Every footfall and hand placement must be carefully considered, especially when negotiating multiple ladders lashed together and extended over bottomless gaps in the ice. Any slip or loss of balance could send a climber tumbling into a crevasse or barreling down the mountain.

In 2001, Erik Weihenmayer made his way through the icefall unharmed, and several days later stood atop the highest mountain in the world. It was an awesome feat for anyone, certainly, but Erik is blind. He is also one of the most accomplished adventurers on the planet. In 2014, he solo kayaked 277 miles of the Grand Canyon. In 2000, he rode his mountain bike from San Francisco to Denver. In 2008, he climbed Carstensz Pyramid in Indonesia, becoming the first blind person to reach the highest point on each of the seven continents. He's also rock climbed the Nose on El Capitan in Yosemite National Park, completed a 457-mile adventure race, and made 50 solo skydives. For each of his adventures, Erik has a support team that uses ingenious ways of communicating with him and helping him through the obstacles and challenges along the way. But Erik also relies on a unique sensory system called echolocation.

Echolocation is a type of sonar whereby a person, or animal in the case of bats and dolphins, emits a call into the environment and then listens for the echo. The tone of the echo provides the information they need to know the size, shape, and distance of objects in the area. With just a click of the tongue, Erik is able to visualize the location of trees, houses, parked cars, and mailboxes while out for a walk in his neighborhood.

The world's foremost expert in human echolocation is Daniel Kish. Blind since the age of one, Daniel has trained himself to "see" buildings as far away as 1,000 feet. He can determine types of cars, and can even tell the difference between a wall and a chain-link fence. In an article by Michael Finkel in *Men's Journal*, Daniel describes how using clicks and interpreting the returning sound waves give him "very rich and very detailed pictures in his head." The sound waves, however, are subtle and take tremendous focus to process. It takes a practiced ear and highly sensitive listening skills to pick out the echo in a sea of ambient noise. People with

sight have this same ability, but because they're able to process images with their eyes, they have no need to tune in to it. They have
no need to listen to the echoes that bombard them every day.

Within the animal kingdom, human beings have excellent
hearing, but rarely do we use our listening skills to their full ca-
pacity. In fact, study after study show that the vast majority of
people don't listen well at all. Their attention tends to shift from
the speaker to the thoughts that are in their head. They become
preoccupied with what they're going to say when it's their turn to
talk or with what they're going to do in the future.

Human beings also think faster than they can talk. So between
pauses, random thoughts can slide in and pull their attention away.
It's also common to get lost in making judgments of the speaker
and whether or not their ideas and positions support our own be-
liefs. In education in particular, where there are so many opposing
philosophies and experiences, listening to others and truly understanding them and their point of view becomes difficult. Being
crunched for time is also a factor, especially in the classroom with
so many students vying to be heard.

My wife and I live on one of several canyons in San Diego. The
canyons, which meander through large tracts of the city, are an oasis
of nature hidden behind houses and within neighborhoods. Although
a stone's throw from popular tourist attractions, many people never
hear of the miles of hiking and biking trails that wind through natural
vegetation and wildlife. From our back deck, we can see raccoons,
coyotes, foxes, and hawks circling the sky above. It's quiet and pleasant—for the most part. Every once in a while, from off in the distance, we'll hear a racket of noise approaching. At first it sounds like
siblings squabbling. It has a complaining, squawking quality to it. As

the cacophony gets closer it becomes loud enough that it will interrupt conversation. It will cause guests to ask, "What is that?" It never fails to bring us out onto the deck for a look.

In bright colors of green and red, San Diego's beach communities are home to several flocks of parrots. How they got here no one knows for sure. Some experts believe they migrated from Mexico, while others say they were once pets who, after being released, began breeding and multiplying. They are a spectacle. Usually in groups of 20 to 30, they fly erratically, darting about every which way but never straying more than a few feet from each other. The only time they seem to quiet down is when, after settling into a tree, they begin munching on flowers and berries.

While flying, though, they all seem to be talking and arguing at the same time. Appropriately, a flock of parrots is also called a pandemonium. According to researchers, they have a highly developed language system. They're able to express sadness, fear, anger, and even surprise with their vocalizations. Somehow, amid all that chaos and noise, they're able to communicate with one another effectively.

Human beings, on the other hand, tend to struggle with listening when there are distractions in the environment. The more you're able to lock in on the speaker with all your senses, the better you'll be able to glean meaning and understanding. This is why it's so important that we remove or pare down distractions in the classroom. We want to give our students the best chance to listen and comprehend what is said. The less that competes for their attention the better. We know this is important. We know this is a key to learning. Improving listening in the classroom is near the top of every teacher's list of priorities. But we rarely hear much about the importance of improving our own listening.

Business, medicine, law, and entertainment are all industries that emphasize good listening and its supreme importance to success. But not teaching. A Google search will turn up perhaps a couple of articles. The fact is, becoming just a little bit better of a listener will make you a much better teacher. It's a lesser-known secret that will also improve your relationships, increase your respect, and make you a lot happier doing your job.

Conventional wisdom says that you improve your listening skills by looking at the speaker, making eye contact, nodding, and paraphrasing. Being empathetic, patient, and impartial are also on the listening to-do list. But focusing on these things can make you feel stilted and unnatural. Although good advice, they can make your interactions feel like work.

The speaker, too, can be thrown off when you're nodding your head again and again and saying "go on" and "what I hear you saying is" like an Adlerian therapist. Inevitably, the burden of having to follow a set of rules every time you engage in conversation will cause you to drop the practice altogether and go back to what comes naturally. Luckily, there is a better way. There is a way to become a better listener without having to snap a rubber band against your wrist every time you interrupt someone or lose your focus.

Richard Branson has successfully founded hundreds of businesses over his career in a wide range of sectors. He began in publishing at the age of 16, interviewing Mick Jagger for a magazine he started called *The Student*. He went on to launch a record label and then an airline before finding success in telecommunications, technology, and banking. His Virgin Group now employs over 60,000 people in dozens of countries around the world. Of his success, Branson often cites the example of his father as one of the best pieces of advice he's ever received. It's advice he's shared again and again in articles and interviews and is the central theme of a book he wrote recently called *The Virgin Way: How to Listen, Learn, Laugh and Lead*. It's advice 18th century novelist Jane Austin might have called just plain, good sense. It is simply to talk less.

Making a conscious decision to do less talking will automatically shut off that voice inside your head imploring you to express your own thoughts, ideas, and opinions. When you resolve just to listen, and not even try to squeeze in your own point of view, it's amazing how much less stress you feel and how much more you learn. I've found it to be one of the best things you can do to experience immediate improvement in your teaching performance and overall job satisfaction.

For starters, talking less and listening more will make you a better colleague. We've all known teachers who have little interest in what anyone else has to say. They dominate grade level and subject matter meetings. They pipe up at every staff meeting. They go on and on with seemingly no awareness that perhaps they should leave some room for others to share. They increase the length of meetings because they must express their every idea and opinion, often just to make themselves look good or feel special.

But what they're actually doing is alienating their colleagues. They're making the collective effort to become a better school for the students and parents in the community more difficult. Their mere presence in a meeting can disrupt, often severely, the learning and collaboration of everyone else. They're hard to communicate with, hard to work with, and hard to like.

Wherever I've taught, I've found that the less you say, the more people admire and respect you and the easier you are to work with. This doesn't mean that you never speak up when you have something helpful or important to say. It doesn't mean that you're rude or that you show disinterest with your body language. It just means that your first inclination, your default position, is to listen and let others do the talking. The benefits are many.

First, your learning skyrockets. When you have no definitive plans to open your mouth, you automatically listen a lot better. You're able to see the big picture and understand the strengths and weaknesses of the latest strategy, method, or teaching approach being discussed. When you do speak, you're able to contribute in a way that sums up, clarifies, simplifies, and benefits everyone involved. Interestingly, when a good listener speaks, people tend to be very respectful. They lean in and listen much better themselves because they know they're going to hear something useful.

One piece of advice you hear again and again when it comes to becoming a better listener is that you must be empathetic. You must put yourself in the speaker's shoes and try to feel what they're feeling. This is certainly important, but the advice can be confusing because empathy is a result of good listening, not the cause. When you resolve not to speak and just to attend to the speaker, you will naturally and without effort begin seeing things from their perspective. Ironically, trying to be empathetic will pull your attention away from good listening.

Another bit of advice you often hear is that you must think before you speak, that if you first stop to consider what you're going to say, then you avoid interrupting or saying something that isn't useful. But again, like empathy, good speaking is a result of good listening, not the result of thinking while others are talking.

Speaking less also makes you appear thoughtful and intelligent. Your quietness communicates that you value other people. You value their time and ideas. You value many points of view, and you value the process of growing together as a staff and school. Because of The Law of Reciprocity, all your interactions will be more polite. Teachers, other staff members, and parents alike will value your time more and be more respectful toward you. You'll find your conversations becoming more pleasant and efficient. Talking less has the effect of giving you more time to organize and prepare and think about your classroom. You'll notice fewer interruptions and almost zero disagreements. Your stress level will plummet and allow you to focus on the job of teaching. The biggest change, though, is that people will look and treat you differently, making your world a happier, more courteous place to be.

Over the years many teachers have asked me how I manage to fly under the radar. They wonder why I never have any drama or personality conflicts. They wonder why it appears that I'm doing a different job altogether, why it seems that I experience the day on a different track, one free from the stress and inconvenience that they experience.

Certainly, the previous 10 chapters account for the lion's share of it. When you're happy and efficient in your job, everything is easier. But the key to staying well respected, and even revered and honored of your time, is a commitment to not talking more than necessary. It's important to note that if you're quiet because you're moody or rude, the aforementioned benefits are off the table. You must make sure you're outwardly polite, that you smile and say hello and take an interest in others. You may also have close friends who you're more loquacious with. But as a general rule, the less you talk, the more satisfied you'll be in your job.

Over the years I've had the chance to observe many classrooms. Teachers will ask me if I can come in and give my thoughts on how they can improve. In almost every case, the first thing I tell them is that they talk too much. Most teachers would benefit greatly by cutting the amount of talking they do by one-third or more.

Some feel the need to fill nearly every moment with reminders, add-ons, and extra advice. They repeat the same directions over and over. They implore and encourage and talk students through every routine and transition. They think out loud and begin speaking without a firm idea about what they want to communicate. They also frequently raise their voice in an effort to be heard and understood. But the more you talk, and the louder you talk, the more your students will tune you out.

The best way to improve listening in your classroom is to talk less. When you're selective with your words, your message will be clearer and more powerful. It will carry with it more meaning and propel action in your students. It also has the effect of making you more likable. You don't waste your students' time or fill the room with unnecessary clutter and tension. When you open your mouth to speak, you give them something that is worth listening to. The result is that focus, concentration, and learning improve. Talking less also frees you to observe and learn more about your students. It frees you to really listen to them, get to know them better, and grow in your relationship. When students feel like they're being heard and have a voice, they relax and settle into the comfortable flow of learning.

In a study at the University of Richmond, researchers Scott Johnson and Curt Bechler found that there was a strong correlation between listening skills and effective leadership. I've certainly found this to be the case in the classroom, but recently I've discovered how important listening is in coaching teachers.

After each session, I analyze my performance. I rate how effectively I was able to communicate to the client precisely what they need to do to transform their teaching experience. Setting aside a few minutes for self-reflection has been one of the best things I've done to ensure I'm providing a good service to the teachers who hire me. Over the course of the past 18 months that I've been offering coaching via Skype, one theme kept popping up. When the client was talkative, and able to express their challenges and frustrations, I was more effective. I was clearer and more detailed in my assessment and prescription for them going forward.

So I made two changes to my coaching practice. First, I created a questionnaire that would better get to the root of their issues. This way, I already had a good idea of the direction I wanted to go with my advice. The second thing I did was resolve to talk a whole lot less. Especially for the first 20 minutes or so, I just listened and encouraged more sharing and expression from them. Not only did this give me the information I needed to reliably and accurately help them improve their classroom, but trust and rapport came much faster and deeper.

During the second half of the session, I could pinpoint and explain exactly what they could do to correct the problems they were experiencing. It underscored for me the remarkable power of talking less and listening more. It was further evidence for why it's so effective in improving relationships, likability, and the ability to be a better teacher to your students and coworker to your colleagues.

I had a blind student in my sixth-grade classroom one year. It was a great experience for everyone. She was bright and funny and challenged everyone around her. She demanded loyal friendship, to the point of hurting feelings. She was passionate about life and unabashed in expressing her opinions. She was well read and shared thoughtful and often touching stories about her life and the books that she loved. But her greatest impact on the classroom was in showing my students, as well as me, what was possible. She was completely fearless and willing to try anything, even at the risk of embarrassment. She made friends with everyone and didn't care who they were or how popular they were. She taught more about maturity and breaking through boundaries than anything I could have done.

She also did things that defied logic. She could recognize me and where I was in the room by the sound of my footsteps, even when I would gleefully try to disguise them (which she loved). She could hear conversations from across the room and would yell out, "I can hear you!" She could also bounce a playground ball right into your hands. Although we may never be able to tap into our ability to listen quite like her or Erik Weihenmayer or Daniel Kish, we can all improve through the habit of talking less.

Maya Angelou once said that if you don't like something, then change it. Resolving to wait and listen first is the change agent that can make you a happier and more effective teacher. It's a prime example of the 80/20 rule. For a small shift in how you communicate, a small adjustment in emphasis from talking to listening, you receive tenfold back in rewards.

Come along
We're settin' sail
Never looking back again

-Audra Day, "The Light That Never Fails"

"It's such a big dream, I can't see it all."

-Edward S. Curtis, author of *The North American Indian*

Seize

Marina Cano is an award-winning wildlife photographer whose work has appeared in publications around the globe. She stands out in a highly competitive field because of her uncanny ability to capture the emotion of her subjects. Her touching photographs of the elephants of Maasai Mara and baby gorillas of Cabárceno, for example, are intimate and personal. They're imbued with a dramatic, portrait-like quality. You get the sense that she was dropped by the hand of God into these gorgeous twinkles of time, place, light, and vulnerability, and then the animals decided to pose for her camera.

In interviews, Cano sprinkles her conversation with words like freedom, peacefulness, and creativity. She talks about living her passion and pursuing the dream she's carried with her since being introduced to photography as a teenager. While on the job, she becomes so immersed in her work that she forgets to eat and loses track of time, which are two hallmarks of *flow* experience.

But wildlife photography isn't a succession of sunsets, rainbows, and profound experiences. In fact, it's one of the toughest and most challenging professions on Earth. Cano spends days out in the bush waiting for a picture that may never come. She sleeps in a tent beneath mosquito netting with ever-present danger lurking just beyond her campsite. She takes malaria pills and hikes mile upon mile in some of the remotest settings in the world, far from medical attention. She spends thousands of dollars of her own money on equipment and safari guides with no guarantee she'll be paid for her work. She is always only as good as her last picture.

Yet, she perseveres. She learns and adjusts. She uses her wits and ingenuity to make her dream a reality. In this way, wildlife photography is like any other career calling. Happiness is never handed to you. You must make it so all by yourself. Even at Google Inc., with its free gourmet food, yoga classes, and hour-long massages, each employee must distinguish themselves among some of the most brilliant minds in the country.

No matter your career path, fulfillment comes only to those who actively pursue it. If you have a wait-and-see approach to your job, and expect the vision you have for yourself thriving and loving your work to miraculously come true, you're liable to be waiting a long time.

The joy of teaching is alive and well, regardless of where you teach. It beats in the heart of every teacher who desires to be more than just a faceless figure students will soon forget. But it's often buried under layers of uncertainty, bad advice, and more and more work and responsibility shoveled onto your plate. Even if you actively pursue it, there is no guarantee you'll find it. Sadly, teacher-training programs do a poor job of preparing students to become real-world teachers. School districts aren't much better. They place most of their emphasis on peripheral details that may contain some value, but have little to do with becoming an effective teacher or inspiring better performance from students.

If you accept everything you hear, implement every strategy you're taught, and chase down every new trend that comes down the pike, then you're in for a long and difficult career. The teachers who are the most stressed-out and unhappy and seeking a career change are those who accept everything they hear as valuable. They try to do the 100 percent, which keeps growing and growing *and growing*, when focusing on the 20 percent that really matters is the key to being effective and happy every day you teach.

Nate Villanueva tried to do it all. He first went into teaching six years ago in order to escape the business-world rat race. A former insurance seller, he dreamed of being Robin Williams' John Keating in *Dead Poets Society*, spurring students to "seize the day." He dreamed of inspiring the next generation and satisfying his subject matter passion. He dreamed of summers off, carefree vacations, and spending more time with his family.

He knew that teaching wasn't going to be easy, but he was unprepared for the long hours and stress that were now closing in on him and crushing his spirit. The students were a greater challenge than he imagined. He struggled with misbehavior, inattentiveness, and low motivation. He found himself becoming angry and raising his voice and being the teacher he swore he would never become.

To have all this wonderful knowledge that he so badly wanted to impart bottled up inside because he didn't know how to get it out was the ultimate frustration. The worst of it, though, was that his teaching career was affecting his home life. He was grading papers and preparing in the evenings and on the weekends. He was tossing and turning at night, cycling through possible solutions to dozens of classroom issues. He was testy around his wife and two children and was considering a return to the comparatively halcyon days of selling insurance. Teaching was becoming a source of resentment rather than the joy he so wanted it to be.

Nate contacted me while just barely hanging on to the last few strands of the end of his rope. Over the course of three coaching sessions, I laid out for Nate what has become this book. We talked about cutting his preparation time by learning to say no and simplifying his lessons. We talked about improving behavior by de-cluttering, shifting responsibility, and influencing students *to want* to learn and behave. We talked about creating inspirational lessons that freed him to be John Keating and Jessica Mendoza rolled into one. We talked about visualization, improvisation, and storytelling. We talked about eliminating stress, heading home at a decent hour, and being the kind of teacher that parents, fellow teachers, and administrators respect and admire.

Like many teachers I coach, during each of our sessions there were moments when Nate had to stop and grab a tissue. Putting words to feelings and realizing just how bad things had gotten has a way of doing that. So too does the hope that there was an answer to his prayers. The 10 preceding chapters will allow anyone to filter out all the unhelpful messages and advice teachers are bombarded with every week and focus on what really works in the classroom. Nate would drop his head and wipe tears from his eyes because I told him that not only did he not have to do more, but I was rec-ommending he do a lot less.

After signing off for the last time with me, I was sorry to see him go. Like many teachers, Nate had so much wisdom and passion to offer his students, but just didn't know how to go about imparting it. I felt certain, though, that Nate now had the tools to create the career he wanted. He now had the strategies and shortcuts to not only make a lifetime impact on his students, but to love (almost) every minute of it. He also now had the time to enjoy the family he so dearly loved, and even take up a new hobby or two. If I could have, I would have been standing right alongside him for the first few weeks of his new approach to teaching.

Often, a client will hire me for a follow-up session three or four weeks later, and I'll find myself doing nothing more than reassuring, confirming, and reiterating what I told them during the previous session. This book gives you the habits shared by great teachers the world over, but you have to put them to use. You have to apply them. You have to cut out the fluff, reassess what you've been doing, and follow the advice. The opportunity is there. But you must seize it.

I heard from Nate a few weeks later, and he was ecstatic. Although he had a few missteps in the beginning, he was now loving his job, inspiring his students, and spending a lot more time with his family. He was living his dream.

Focusing on the happy habits detailed in this book doesn't mean that you'll ignore parts of your curriculum. It doesn't mean that you'll fail to complete mandated assignments and deadlines or that you'll stray off schedule. The habits in this book give you a focus through which you can incorporate whatever curriculum or materials you've been asked to use. They are designed this way. They are designed to give you an enduring foundation upon which you can build an effective and fulfilling career, regardless of grade level, subject matter, or school district you work for. You'll filter what you learn in professional books, trainings, and staff meetings through the lens of your new habits. You'll have a good sense of what to incorporate, if anything, and how to incorporate it.

It's important to note that implementing the happy teacher habits isn't like beginning an exercise or diet program, which can take great willpower to develop into habits. In his book, *The Power of Habit*, Charles Duhigg points out that habits emerge naturally as the result of our brain looking for ways to save effort. We take the path of least resistance. We create routines that free us to think about more important things.

The happy teacher habits do this on every account. They make life easier and more efficient. They allow your creative powers to be used for what is essential rather than what is trivial. They save mental and physical energy by focusing on just the few things that make the greatest impact. Hence, they require far less willpower than cutting sweets from your diet or beginning that novel you've always wanted to write.

They constitute the roadmap teachers are desperately looking for, and thus you'll be able to dive in and create your new habits without looking back. I've seen this over and over again with the teachers I've coached and mentored over the years. Once you begin to see the difference the happy teacher habits make in both your personal and professional life, continuing to use them is something you'll never have to consciously think about. Experiencing success and deepening fulfillment is the greatest hedge against going back to your old ways of doing things. But you still must take that first step.

I recommend starting slowly and rolling out each new habit in the order they are presented. Spend a few days saying no before tidying up your classroom. Get comfortable with improvisation before focusing too heavily on shifting responsibility. You'll find, however, that each habit supports and strengthens the rest, particularly those that involve preparing and carrying out inspiring lessons. Each habit, on its own, can and will make you a better teacher. But it's the collective force of all that will deliver the gift of extraordinary teaching.

As you carve out more time, and as your energy and enjoyment begin to rise, you'll become better and better at teaching until one day in the not too distant future, you'll have the feeling that you've arrived. You'll feel like you really do understand the job and how to sift through the mountains of information that are thrown at you. You'll feel like you can walk into any classroom in the world and create a learning experience your students will love being part of.

In teaching circles, however, you've no doubt heard again and again how there is always so much to learn. You've heard again and again that you're not good enough, that you'll never arrive, and that you must continue to add to your repertoire of professional knowledge and strategies.

It's good to be aware of what's out there, without question. It's good to know what politicians and curriculum writers are hawking. It's good to know what the research *really* says, and where it comes from. But good teaching is enduring. Good teachers are good their whole career. It doesn't matter what comes down the pike or how many changes they have to deal with. Bill Heyde, my high school English teacher who you met in chapter eight, is now retired. But I have no doubt that you could drop him into any time in history, and he'd still be a most remarkable and inspiring teacher. He'd still have his students laughing, learning, and sitting on the edge of their seats.

Amid the bronze helmets, ornate metopes, statues, columns, and other treasures that fill the Archaeological Museum of Olympia, sits a piece of exercise equipment that is over 2,000 years old and is still in use today. In a multi-billion dollar industry kept alive by trends that come and go, the kettlebell endures. Made of cast iron, the kettlebell is shaped like a cannonball with a thick handle attached to the top. It costs $1.50 or so per pound and can be used in an area the size of a small bathroom. Swung, pulled, and pushed overhead, the kettlebell is both a strength and cardiovascular exercise in one.

It improves flexibility and balance. It strengthens the core muscles of the back and abdominals. It shapes muscles, burns calories, and lowers blood pressure. It can be used by beginner and advanced practitioners alike, and because of the many and varied movements and rotations available, every day can feel like a fresh new workout. It is the essence of efficiency. After century upon century, it's never been improved upon. Yet, every year millions of people spend hundreds of dollars looking for the next best thing. Fitness is an 11 billion dollar industry predicated on selling the public expensive programs and equipment they don't need and will rarely use.

Like barre classes, Zumba DVDs, and the Fitbit, new curriculums, programs, and technologies are fine and good, and I don't disparage anyone who earnestly seeks to improve education. But it is the skill of individual teachers to inspire students that will always have the greatest impact. A school full of happy teachers who *know* how to manage students and crank up their motivational engines is more potent than a thousand new computers and more impactful than whether 50 percent or 75 percent of instructional time is spent on non-fiction texts.

By focusing on the happy teacher habits to become an extraordinary teacher, all the other stuff will fall into place. Their importance will drop way down on your priority list. Your teaching life will be simplified and the goals for your students will be straightforward. Professional trainings, conferences, and staff meetings will no longer be a source of frustration. Your skeptical ear will be able to recognize what really matters in the bright light of your new habits. You'll find them unaffected by changes to curriculum, schedules, or anything else. Whether it's a new reading program, math approach, or emphasis on project-based learning, none of it will alter the core foundations of good teaching.

In the summer of 1900, photographer Edward S. Curtis accompanied anthropologist and *Forest and Stream* editor George Bird Grinnell on an expedition to northern Montana. They were hoping to witness one of the last known performances of the Sun Dance, a sacred religious ceremony of the Blackfoot and Piegan tribes. As they led their horses over a mountain pass near their destination, they came upon a scene so breathtaking that it would alter the course of Curtis' life.

Spread out before them on the valley floor below were over a thousand teepees and countless men, women, and children going about their daily chores and amusements. Over the next few days, having witnessed the strength and dignity of the people, Curtis resolved to record with his camera and pen the life and traditions of Native Americans before they disappeared.

In a letter to Grinnell shortly after returning from the expedition, Curtis wrote, "I am a poor man, but I've got my health, plenty of steam, and something to work for." For the next 30 years, he pursued his passion and his purpose. His culminating work, *The North American Indian*, contains 20 volumes of thousands of photos and pages of text documenting the lives of more than 80 North American nations. By the time of its publishing in 1930, little would remain of these great tribes and the traditions they lived and died for.

Like Marina Cano, many of Curtis' photos are intimate portraits. Perusing the hundreds upon hundreds of individual images, you can't help but be affected by these proud people adorned in their finest clothing, headdresses, and ornamentation. Curtis cared deeply for his subjects, and their dignity shines through, above all.

There are also photographs of everyday life—hunting, fishing, eating, weaving, and caring for children. But for me, one picture stands out above the rest. It's a snapshot of a chief or elder of the Crow tribe, sitting horseback atop a hill. His headdress reaches all the way past his heels. He is shirtless and holds a bow and several arrows in his left hand. His right hand is clenched behind the string, with an arrow at the ready. There is also an arrow between his teeth.

The photo is called, *Ready for the Charge* and it hangs in my living room. It's a beautiful photograph, but it's the look on the chief's face that first drew me in. His head is canted slightly upward. His eyes are on the horizon. The sunshine is on his face. He appears content, but also determined to do what he must do and fulfill his destiny. It's an image that represents for me Edward Curtis, Marina Cano, and anyone else who doggedly pursues their calling in life. It represents every teacher who gets up each morning determined to make a difference.

Happiness in teaching doesn't mean that you'll always have a smile on your face. It doesn't mean you won't have to make tough decisions or be involved in heartbreaking situations. It does mean, however, that you'll have a definitive path to follow. It means that you'll have the knowledge and skill to make an impact on your students that will last a lifetime, like a photograph that never fades. It means that you'll have time for a life outside of school—to build a family, enjoy other interests and passions, or sit and relish the quiet of an evening at home.

The opportunity is there to have the teaching experience you desire, but it's not going to come to you. No one is going to hold your hand or come to your rescue. You have to climb up on that horse all by yourself, lift your eyes to the horizon, and go get it.

The Happy Teacher Habits

1. **Narrow** - Focus on the 20 percent that makes the biggest difference in your happiness and teaching success.

2. **Decline** - Say no to anything that pulls you away or distracts you from the 20 percent that really matters.

3. **Tidy** - Remove all clutter from your classroom. Organize and tidy until it reflects your expectations of excellence.

4. **Inspire** - Rid your classroom of external rewards. Instead, create an environment that encourages intrinsic motivation.

5. **Improvise** - Be an expert in your content area and lean on your natural ability to improvise.

6. **Bridge** - Use the three-step planning process to bridge the gap between your curriculum and the hearts and minds of your students.

7. **Envision** - Visualize your lessons, your responses to misbehavior, and the sequence of each day.

8. **Shift** - Teach great lessons and then shift responsibility in total to your students.

9. **Sway** - Build trust and influence by being consistently pleasant and relying on your classroom management plan.

10. **Listen** - Be a better, stronger leader and colleague by talking less and listening more.

11. **Seize** - True happiness in teaching isn't going to fall into your lap. You must take it for yourself.

References/Further Reading

The 80/20 Principle: The Secret to Achieving More with Less
Richard Koch

Blink: The Power of Thinking Without Thinking
Malcolm Gladwell

The Creative Habit: Learn It and Use It for Life
Twyla Tharp

The Daffodil Principle
Jaroldeen Asplund Edwards

Drive: The Surprising Truth About What Motivates Us
Daniel H. Pink

Essentialism: The Disciplined Pursuit of Less
Greg McKeown

Everest: Mountain Without Mercy
Broughton Coburn

Flow: The Psychology of Optimal Experience
Mihaly Csikszentmihalyi

Grit: The Power of Passion and Perseverance
Angela Duckworth

A Higher Call: An Incredible True Story of Combat and Chivalry in the War-Torn Skies of World War II
Adam Makos

Improv Wisdom: Don't Prepare, Just Show Up
Patricia Ryan Madson

Joel Sternfeld: Walking the High Line
Joel Sternfeld

The Last Place on Earth: Scott and Amundsen's Race to the South Pole
Roland Huntford

Lean In: Women, Work, and the Will to Lead
Sheryl Sandberg

The Life-Changing Magic of Tidying Up: The Japanese Art of Decluttering and Organizing
Marie Kondo

Longitude: The True Story of a Lone Genius Who Solved the Greatest Scientific Problem of His Time
Dava Sobel

Mindset: The New Psychology of Success
Carol S. Dweck

The Narcissism Epidemic: Living in the Age of Entitlement
Jean M. Twenge and W. Keith Campbell

The North American Indian
Edward S. Curtis

The Obstacle Is the Way: The Timeless Art of Turning Trials into Triumph
Ryan Holiday

The ONE Thing: The Surprisingly Simple Truth Behind Extraordinary Results
Gary Keller and Jay Papasan

Parkinson's Law, and Other Studies in Administration
Cyril Northcote Parkinson

The Power of Habit: Why We Do What We Do in Life and Business
Charles Duhigg

Quiet: The Power of Introverts in a World That Can't Stop Talking
Susan Cain

The Rise: Creativity, the Gift of Failure, and the Search for Mastery
Sarah Lewis

The Rise of Superman: Decoding the Science of Ultimate Human Performance
Steven Kotler

Smartcuts: How Hackers, Innovators, and Icons Accelerate Success
Shane Snow

Talent is Overrated: What Really Separates World-Class Performers from Everybody Else
Geoff Colvin

Total Immersion: The Revolutionary Way to Swim Better, Faster, and Easier
Terry Laughlin

Touch the Top of the World: A Blind Man's Journey to Climb Farther Than the Eye Can See
Erik Weihenmayer

The Virgin Way: How to Listen, Learn, Laugh and Lead
Richard Branson

The War of Art: Break Through the Blocks and Win Your Inner Creative Battles
Steven Pressfield

The Wright Brothers
David McCullough

For free classroom management tips, strategies, and solutions, sign up for our newsletter at smartclassroommanagement.com

Made in the USA
Lexington, KY
01 May 2016